Knock, Knock, Who's There?

Knock, Knock, Who's There?

ELIZABETH
WINTHROP

Holiday House · *New York*

for Mudge, with thanks and love

Library of Congress Cataloging in Publication Data

Winthrop, Elizabeth.
    Knock, knock, who's there?

    SUMMARY: Two brothers and their mother each
try in their own way to come to terms with the
father's death and in the process learn to cope
with a disease that threatens to cripple all of
them.
    [1. Family problems—Fiction. 2. Death—
Fiction. 3. Alcoholism—Fiction] I. Title.
PZ7.W768Kn   [Fic]   78-6992
ISBN 0-8234-0337-8

1

Sam knew that if he leaned out far enough he could touch it. Run his hand along the shiny new wood, over the brass hinges. Reach out and try to touch him just one more time.

"When someone dies, Pa, where do they go?" He had asked that question long ago, back when he thought his father would never die.

"Nobody knows, Sam. To some kind of heaven or hell, maybe. Or to nothing at all. Their bodies go into the ground. Dust to dust."

I want to know where he is, Sam thought. I know his body is in that box, eyes closed, hands folded. But where's his laugh and his story-telling voice and why does Michael run away all the time and what is Ma thinking when she looks at me with that vague, lost expression in her eyes? He began to shake, first his hands and then his legs and then his chest. Someone took his hand and held it tight, and he finally let go and cried. He didn't care that the church was full of people and he was sixteen years old and standing in the front pew and that everybody told him to be brave for his mother's sake. He stood there and let the stupid tears come out.

Then he was singing with everybody else. Pa had picked out the hymn himself. "I want that Easter hymn, Deborah. I want to believe that I'll be going to a better world than this one." And Ma had nodded, her bottom lip clenched between her teeth because she always said she didn't want him to see her crying.

"'The strife is o'er, the battle done, the victory of life is won, the song of triumph has begun. Alleluia.'"

Six of them carried the coffin out. "No wheels," Ma had told the undertaker. "His sons and friends are strong enough to carry him." Sam and Michael were in the middle on either side. Sam felt an odd sense of relief that at last he was doing something for Pa after all those months of sickness.

* * *

"I wish I could do something for you."

Pa smiled. "It's good to have you here. I like the company." He shifted his position in the bed. The movements under the sheets were slow and painful.

"Do you want another pillow?" Sam asked.

"No. I'm fine." They were silent for a while. "I just wish I didn't feel so tired, Sam. I'd like to have the energy to take a walk with you. A quick turn around the square. See what the view is like from the monument."

"We'll have time for that, Pa. Once you've kicked this pneumonia, you'll be your old self again. Just like last fall."

"I hope so, Sam." They didn't look at each other. "Open the window for a minute. Tell me what's going on up at the monument."

Sam leaned out and looked up the street toward the square. The weather had grown warmer in the last few days so the streets were bare of snow for the first time since November. The family had moved to Charlestown from Beacon Hill when Sam was twelve. His father had bought and renovated an old rooming house. Pa was a doctor but his hobbies were history and architecture.

"A lot of people are out today," Pa said. "I can hear their voices."

"It's so warm for January," Sam answered, pulling his head inside and closing the window. "All the kids are up at the square. Just like those spring afternoons when they play baseball in that triangle beside the steps."

"Who's there?"

Sam shrugged. "The Irish kids. All Michael's friends."

"Where is Michael?" Pa asked. "I never see him anymore."

"He's all wrapped up in that drama group down at the church," Sam muttered.

"He told me about that," Pa said quietly. "I had forgotten." He leaned his head back against the pillow and closed his eyes. Sam studied the drawn face. His father had lost so much weight that the bones in his cheeks and his jaw seemed too large. His hair had gotten gray just around his ears. It's not fair, Sam thought to himself for the hundredth time. Why should it be Pa? What will I do if he dies?

Pa had opened his eyes and was looking at him. "What are you thinking about, Sam?"

Sam shifted uneasily in his seat. He didn't answer. There were questions he wanted to ask but the words were hard to say. Pa spoke first.

"I was remembering the time we retraced the route the British soldiers took during the Battle of Bunker Hill. Kathleen was with us that time, wasn't she?"

Sam nodded. "She always came along on those tours—" Sam stopped. He had meant to say comes, but

Pa didn't seem to notice. He was staring up at the ceiling.

"Remember Mr. O'Donnell's face when we marched right through his backyard when he was weeding the flower patch?" Pa asked. "Right over the fence, across the lawn, and out the other side."

Sam laughed.

"I have all my history books downstairs in the same place, Sam. I want you to keep reading them. Together you and Kathleen probably know more about the history of Charlestown than anybody else who lives here." He paused. "All this time lying here in bed. I don't even have the energy to read anymore." He closed his eyes. Sam stood up and walked over to the bureau. On either side of the mirror, Ma had hung two rows of family pictures. There was Pa in his navy uniform standing on the bridge of the ship. Pa holding the baby Sam on christening day, with Ma in the background looking shy and nervous. Sam and Michael on the sea wall in front of the house in Maine, right next to a picture of Pa as a little boy sitting in the same place.

"Bring me that one," Pa said from behind him. "The one of you two boys on the wall."

Sam handed it to him, and they looked at it in silence for a minute. "Michael looks older than me," Sam remarked. "He always does."

Pa laughed softly. "You shouldn't worry about that, Sammy. It will even out in the end." He pointed to a corner of the picture. "I always loved that funny dormer window on the third floor of the house. It looked like such an afterthought to me."

"I can't believe we're never going there again," Sam blurted out. "It seems so wrong to have someone else living in our house."

Pa handed him the picture and he hung it back in its place. "We *had* to sell the house. A person in my position

8

has to get his affairs in order." He looked at Sam. "It just doesn't make sense to leave something like that for your mother to do later. Afterwards."

Sam felt a lump pushing up in his throat. He wanted suddenly to go to his father and hug him but something held him back. He had not touched his father since he was a little boy.

"Sam, come sit by me," Pa said softly. He moved over in the bed, and Sam propped himself up next to his father's thin body. It felt good to be close to him and yet he held himself very still, scared that any movement might bruise Pa's fragile bones.

Pa took his hand and held it tight.

"There's not much time left now, Sam," he whispered.

"Pa, don't say that please."

"Sam, I need to talk to someone. I can't go on pretending something that isn't true."

There was a long silence. Outside Sam could hear the shouts of the kids up at the monument.

"Are you scared, Pa?" Sam whispered.

"Scared of dying?" Pa asked. "Not anymore, I guess. I don't want to die, God knows. I'm too young. For a while, when Dr. Chambers first told me what I had, I was just angry. Then I refused to believe it. That was last spring when I played tennis every afternoon even though my blood counts were so low." He smiled. "Your mother was furious with me. Now I'm just plain tired. I'm too tired to read, I'm too tired to walk, I'm too tired to eat. I'm too tired to even fight this disease anymore."

"Pa, don't say that," Sam cried. "It's just this pneumonia that's got you down. Dr. Chambers says the antibiotics are working."

"But if I get through this, there'll always be another infection. I just don't have the blood anymore to back it all up. Remember what I told you about this disease.

With pernicious anemia, the blood just slowly turns to water." He reached up and ran both hands through his hair, a familiar gesture. "When you're as sick as I am, Sammy, there comes a time when you accept that you're going to die. Maybe not tomorrow, maybe not next month, but sooner than you should." He stared off into space. "That time has come for me. I'm not angry anymore. I don't want to fight it anymore. I feel a strange sense of peace inside." When he looked at Sam, there were tears in his eyes. "I wish you could all feel peaceful with me."

Sam didn't say anything. He stared down at the floor, willing himself not to cry, holding Pa's hand as tight as he dared. Downstairs, they heard the front doorbell.

"That will be Mrs. Fitzhugh with the blood transfusion," Pa said. Ma opened the bedroom door just as Sam stood up. She came over to the bed and straightened out the covers.

"Sam, can you answer the door, please?"

He went out of the room, but instead of going right downstairs, he stood on the landing and watched his parents for a minute. Ma took a hairbrush and brushed his father's hair just the way she used to do for Sam when he was a little boy. Then she leaned over and kissed him quickly on the lips. Sam turned away. It was Ma that had kept them all going through this, no matter how bad it had been. There was something so direct and matter-of-fact about the way she handled Pa. "We're not going to think about tomorrow and next week and next year," she once told Sam when they first learned how sick Pa was. "We're just going to take every day and do our best with that. That's the only way we can help him get better."

The doorbell rang again, and Sam went down to let the nurse in.

* * *

Now Sam watched the long line of cars leave the cemetery. Only a few people came back to the house, where Aunt Holly had put out some food in the downstairs dining room. The first-floor rooms had been furnished formally, and even though Pa was proud of the way everything looked, he and Ma preferred to eat in the big bright kitchen on the second floor. The family really lived on the top two floors of the house.

"Aunt Holly still thinks she's over on Beacon Hill," Michael whispered in Sam's ear. "Everything looks so formal and correct."

"She wanted everybody to go back to their house but Ma blew up. Aunt Holly always has hated Charlestown," Sam said.

"It's such a—a backwater," Michael spluttered, imitating Aunt Holly's high-pitched voice.

Kathleen was waiting at the top of the stairs when Sam and Michael came in. She was an Irish girl who lived across the street in one of the old row houses that had never been renovated. She and Sam had become good friends when the Everetts first moved to Charlestown. That was when Kathleen used to baby-sit for Michael. She had been fascinated by the house and the way the Everetts lived. "It's so quiet here," she'd told Sam once. "Like a church. In our house, somebody is always yelling."

"Why are you hiding up there?" Michael called to her. She waved at them to come up.

"I don't think your mother wants me here," she said quietly.

"So what?" Michael said. "We want you here."

There was a sudden silence between the three of them. They had not been together much lately.

"How was it?" she asked.

Michael flopped down on the stairs. "It made me angry," he said.

"Me too," said Sam. "I wanted to know—" He stopped.

"What?" Kathleen asked.

"It sounds crazy . . ." Sam muttered.

There was another silence. From downstairs, Sam could hear the low rumble of voices and the clink of forks.

"How can they eat?" Michael said. "They're all acting like it's a wedding or something. That's what makes me so mad. All those people singing and crying and looking pious. And tomorrow, it will all be forgotten. We're the ones who have to live with it."

"You're angry because of the other people," Sam said. "I'm angry because I don't know where he's gone."

"Underground," said Michael sarcastically. "You were there when they lowered the coffin."

"Oh, shut up, Michael."

"What do you mean, Sam?" Kathleen asked. "About not knowing where he's gone."

Sam didn't answer her question. He would tell her sometime. But not in front of Michael.

"Boys, I think you should come down and say good-bye to some of your father's friends." Aunt Holly's face peered up the steep stairs at them.

"We're coming," Sam called. She disappeared down the hall.

"Who's that?" Kathleen asked.

"Aunt Holly. Uncle Theodore's wife. She's Pa's older sister. The bossy one," Michael said.

"Why didn't you come to the church?" Sam asked Kathleen. He remembered sitting in the front pew, trying to imagine where she was sitting, wondering if she'd found the church. But later when he was waiting in the black car and watching the people stream out the doors, he knew suddenly that she hadn't come.

"My mother wouldn't let me," she said. "She said it was too far." She glanced down at her hands. The long dark hair fell in front of her shoulder so that he couldn't see her face. "I wanted to come," she said softly.

"That's a crazy excuse. You go farther than that to college every day," Sam said.

She shrugged. "Mum didn't think it was right for me to go there. I mean, with all those important people."

"Pa would have liked it," Sam said coldly.

"Leave her alone, Sam," Michael muttered. "Pa wasn't her father. Come on, Kathleen."

They went downstairs together, leaving Sam huddled at the top. He put his forehead down on his knees and stared into the darkness. He felt tired and sick and small again, just like the little boy who had run away for a whole summer's night in the Maine woods.

"Why did you go?" Pa had asked the next morning when he climbed back up the porch steps, feeling stiff and a little silly.

"You and Ma were so angry. I could hear you shouting through the walls. Why were you fighting?"

Pa had not answered. Sam remembered now the hard, tired look that had passed across his father's face. "I'll tell you some other time, Sam," he'd said. "When you are older." But he never did.

I should have asked him the question again, Sam thought now as he saw the drawn face of his mother coming slowly toward him up the stairs.

2

Michael was up in his room when the doorbell rang. He knew Sam had gone downtown with Ma to the lawyer's office so he was alone in the house. He ran down the two flights of stairs. Aunt Holly was standing outside, holding two suitcases.

"Good morning, Michael," she said crisply as she walked past him. "Your mother is out, isn't she?"

"Yes, she's down at the lawyer's office."

"Good. I wanted to come when she wasn't here," she said as she headed up the stairs. Michael followed slowly. When he got upstairs, he found her in his parents' bedroom, emptying some of the bureau drawers.

"What are you doing?" he asked in a bewildered voice.

"I'm taking away your father's clothes." She picked up a pile of his sweaters and placed them neatly in the suitcase. "I wanted to save your mother this job. It would be too painful for her to have to go through all these things."

"How do you know?" Michael asked. "Does she know you're doing this?"

"No, Michael," Aunt Holly said. "I don't want her to have to worry about it."

"You can't just take all those clothes away without telling her. Sam's almost big enough to wear some of Pa's things. Where are you taking them?"

She glanced up at him, surprised by the rude tone in his voice. "The clothes will be at our house when Sam wants them," she explained quietly. "Now, please stop shouting at me."

Michael stood silently, watching her hands pulling, patting, and folding his father's shirts and socks. He shivered.

"Your father certainly did know how to destroy his clothes," Aunt Holly said as she refolded a ripped shirt. "I think I'll just give some of these things to the church."

"You can't do that without asking Ma," Michael shouted. "You shouldn't even be touching Pa's things."

"Michael, just calm down. You're getting too excited." She snapped one suitcase shut. "Now please take this down for me. The car is parked right outside the door."

"I won't touch it," Michael said. He turned and ran upstairs to his room, slamming the door behind him.

Ma and Sam found Michael in the kitchen when they got home.

"Aunt Holly was here," Michael said quietly to Ma.

"She said she was going to leave some food for us," Ma said, taking off her coat and throwing it over the chair. She sat down and pulled off her wet boots. "It's horrible out," she said. Sam slumped into another chair.

"She took Pa's clothes away," Michael said.

Ma stopped moving.

"She what?" Sam asked. Michael was still looking at his mother.

"She took everything, all his old sweaters with the

holes, and his suits. Even the socks. She said it would make you feel better."

"That goddamned bitch," Ma said as she got up from the table and walked out of the room, one shiny boot still dangling from her hand. She slammed the bedroom door behind her.

"How could you let her do that?" Sam asked.

Michael stood up suddenly, throwing his chair over onto the floor. "What was I supposed to do, lock her in the house?" For the first time since Pa died, Michael felt suddenly like crying. He walked out of the kitchen and started slowly up the stairs. Halfway up, he stopped. "Hey, Sam," he called.

"What?"

"How could you let Pa do that?" he asked.

"Do what?" Sam said.

"Die," Michael answered. Then he continued up to his room away from the stunned silence.

"Did you talk to Aunt Holly?" Michael asked his mother the next morning at breakfast.

"I called her." Ma shrugged. "She was trying to help."

"She looked like a vulture, picking over Pa's things that way," Michael said.

Ma looked at him blankly. "She will keep his clothes there until you boys want them."

"I don't want them," Sam said sharply. "I'm not going over there to get his things."

"Who does she think—" Michael started.

"Please stop," Ma said, raising her hand. Her voice sounded like glass breaking. Sharp and final. "Please let's not talk about it anymore." They slipped into a vacant silence, eyes down, fingers fiddling with spoons and threads and bits of nothing. Michael pushed out his chair with an angry scrape.

16

"Where are you going?" Sam asked.

"Out," he answered and was gone.

Michael unlocked the auditorium door and pushed it open slowly. The room was dark, but his hand went easily to the light switches and flicked them on, one after another along the line. He stood and looked around the familiar room. He had joined the church drama group that first summer Pa was sick when they had to come home early from Maine. Since then, he had spent more time down here than at home. Father Fitzgerald had given him a key after he found him waiting on the steps for the third afternoon in a row.

"Come and go when you want," the priest had said with a smile. "If there's someone using the place, I'm sure they won't mind you going in and out. Just be sure to lock up if you're the last one out."

The kids in the neighborhood all liked Father Fitzgerald because he trusted them. He had grown up in Charlestown. "When I was a kid, I wanted to be a boxer," he told Michael. "I loved to fight. One fall we roped off part of the monument grounds and held regular contests every Saturday afternoon. The cops left us alone. They even stopped sometimes and put their money down on one or another of us. I would have gone on to be a boxer but I got sidetracked."

He had gone away to the seminary. After he'd served in parishes in the Midwest and California, the church had sent him back home to Charlestown. "I didn't want to come. I knew what this place was like. It would be tougher than anything else, trying to change the people who knew me so well."

Michael walked up to the stage and slowly pulled open the dark green curtains that were musty and torn in two places. The stage was big, built in the days when St.

Mary's was a richer parish. Michael stood in the center of the dark space and looked out over the rows of empty seats, imagining the faces watching him. He knew his lines better than anybody else because he spent so much time here reciting them.

There were about ten kids who came to the church regularly for drama classes and about ten others who drifted in and out when they felt like it. People were always coming in late and leaving late, but the banging of the door never seemed to bother Father Fitzgerald. He was often late himself.

Michael walked around slowly, turning on the stage lights and putting out the chairs. The side door opened and Kevin and Patrick came in, followed by Molly, a friend of Kathleen's, and Andrew, Kathleen's younger brother. They all trooped up onto the stage.

"Is Father here yet?" Patrick asked.

"Not yet," Michael said. "He told me something about a meeting with the bishop this morning."

"That means trouble," Molly said. "The bishop is mad about the fact that the attendance at St. Mary's has dropped since Father Fitzgerald came here."

"What's the problem with everybody?" Michael asked. "Don't they like the sermons?"

Patrick burst out laughing, and Michael knew he had said something foolish.

"The local priest's supposed to build up the congregation," Molly explained. "Father Fitzgerald cares more about what happens to us kids than who arranges the altar flowers. Our parents are pretty mad at him. He's always telling us we have to get more education, that we have to get out of Charlestown. Like Kathleen Murphy going to college."

Michael nodded. He remembered what a stink the Murphys had made over that. Pa had written a recommendation to help her get into Boston College. "Mum keeps telling me she never needed college," Kathleen told Sam and Michael. "Mum wants me to get married and get pregnant, just the way she did."

"So anyway, people are staying away from the church, and they've stopped giving money and that makes the bishop mad," Patrick said. "He doesn't care what Father Fitzgerald is doing for us kids. He just wants the people here to support the church."

"Maybe you guys should start going to church," Michael said with a grin.

"Very funny," Kevin said.

"That's not a bad idea," Molly said. "But we don't have the money to drop in the basket, and that's what really counts."

Some more people began trooping in, and after waiting around for a while, they decided to start the rehearsal without the priest. He came in just as they were finishing the first act.

"I'm glad you started without me," he said, pulling off his boots and dropping them under a chair. The wet snow slid off them and melted in a dirty puddle on the floor. "Why don't you just start the first act and run through it again without stopping?"

Kevin groaned. "We just finished doing the first act."

"Good," said the priest. "Then it won't be too hard to do over."

The actors took their places and started in again. Father Fitzgerald took a seat in the front row and listened for a while.

"Stop, everybody," he shouted after Molly had finished a long speech.

"I thought you weren't going to stop us," Patrick said. He collapsed into the nearest chair.

"Well, I'm not going to let you go on mumbling to

each other for a whole hour. First of all, I can't understand a word that any of you are saying, and I can't tell whether you haven't learned your lines or you just don't want the audience to hear the play."

"I don't like all this old-fashioned language," Kevin grumbled. "All these 'ayes' and 'me thinks.' It sounds ridiculous."

Father Fitzgerald ignored his remark. He walked up onto the stage. "You've got to think about your characters more. Now, Molly, Pegeen is a saucy young barmaid who has chosen to marry Shawn Keogh just because there's nothing better around. She's not happy with the situation, but when her father ridicules Shawn, she's got to defend him more vehemently. After all, he's her future husband. Don't sound so listless in that scene when you snatch the shirt from Andrew. All right, try it again from when Shawn goes out the door."

They went through the scene again, and Father Fitzgerald waved at them to keep going, but it wasn't long before he jumped up and stopped the action again.

"Patrick, when Christy first comes into the bar, he is tired and cold and scared that these people are going to turn him over to the police for hitting his father. It's only later when he sees they're in awe of him that he becomes such a terrible braggart. So don't come into the tavern, swaggering and carrying on. You've got to make your entry more humble." He paused and watched Patrick, who was sitting down again. "You don't look too well this morning, Patrick. Where was the party last night?"

Patrick shrugged without answering.

"Next door to us," Molly said quietly. "I could hear them carrying on all night."

"Oh, shut up," Patrick muttered.

"All right, let's just do that one entrance scene again

and then we can call it a day," the priest said. "Michael, you come on again and then Patrick will follow."

When Father Fitzgerald let them go, he called Patrick over and spoke to him quietly. Patrick slammed the door behind him when he left.

"What's wrong with him?" Michael asked.

Father Fitzgerald did not answer for a minute. "I told Patrick he'd be a drunk before he'd ever be an actor if he kept going that way."

"It's not that bad, is it, Father?"

"That's the way it always starts," the priest said as he turned away. "Lock up when you leave, will you, Michael?"

Michael was the last to leave. He walked up the hill past the old training field and stood outside the house for a minute. He had stood there many times before, dreading what news there'd be of Pa's condition, dreading the look of despair on his mother's face, dreading Sam's precise medical questions that carefully avoided the question they were all asking themselves. Is he going to die? And now even though Pa was gone, he still hesitated. Finally, he opened the front door and trudged up the stairs.

3

They went back to school the week after Pa died.

"We've all got to pick up our lives and keep going," Ma said at dinner on Sunday night. "Don't you two worry about me being here alone. I will be just fine."

Her voice had a tone of urgency to it as if she were trying to convince herself more than the two of them. Ma is pretty, Sam realized as he sat watching her across the table. Her dark short hair and her dark eyes seemed to go together, one darkness picking up and framing the other. But her face looked too sharp and thin, her large eyes sunk too deep into the bones from so many nights without sleep. What will she do now? Sam wondered.

The next morning they trudged down the slippery winter hill to the bus stop, the way they had always done. They went to a private school in Beacon Hill because Pa said the public and parochial schools in Charlestown weren't good enough. Michael hated the long ride back and forth. He had once asked Pa if he could go to the public school in Charlestown, and when Pa said no, Michael had shouted, "You don't even know what

Charlestown's really like. The Irish kids say you're a snob."

"That's too bad, Michael, but I'm afraid I don't really care what the 'kids' think. I want you boys to get a good education, and that means you'll have to go to Beacon Hill. It's one of the concessions we've made to live here."

Michael had laughed. "You haven't made any concessions, Pa. Ma and Sam and I are the ones who've given up things."

"Don't talk to your father that way," Ma said sharply.

Michael left the room before anybody could stop him. There had been a silence around the table because, as usual, they had all recognized the uncomfortable truth in what he said.

Grandmother had set up a trust fund to pay for their education. "If you're going to move my grandchildren out to that backwater," she told her son, "I'm at least going to make sure they get a good education."

Old Mrs. Everett had been generous in her own stubborn way. She had lived in a big, old dark house on Beacon Hill, where the family still gathered for holidays and Sunday lunches in the winter. Grandmother never once came to look at the house in Charlestown, even after Grandfather died and she complained of being lonely. "It's too far for me. I'm getting old," she'd say.

"It's not as far as Maine," Pa would remind her gently. Every June she moved up to the house on the Point in Maine where she and Grandfather had spent every summer since they bought the place in the early thirties. She died there one August in the sunny second floor bedroom where the white wispy curtains curled in and out with the breeze off the ocean. In her will, she left the Beacon Hill house to her daughter, Holly, and the house up on the Point to her son.

"She was right about Charlestown," Pa had told Sam

when they walked up to the monument the day after they brought her home to Boston to be buried. "It was too far away in her mind. She never could accept my moving out of the enclave. As far as she was concerned, only Irish immigrants live in Charlestown." She wasn't far off, Sam had thought, but he didn't say it out loud.

Walking down the hill today, Sam glanced sideways at Michael. Nobody would ever guess they were brothers. All the contrasts and disagreements between them seemed to be drawn right into their faces. Where Sam's hair was dark like his mother's, Michael's hair was blond and thin. In a sudden wind it floated around his face like a full and waving halo. Sam's face was thin and sharp-edged, but Michael's was wide and pale and his bright blue eyes looked out in a hard, straight gaze that seemed out of place in that soft face. He dressed well and stood well, and his self-confidence gave Sam a strange ache of loneliness and inadequacy. He could never put the feeling into words.

"You're staring at me," Michael said.

"Sorry," Sam mumbled, looking away.

Michael saw Patrick struggling up the icy hill toward them.

"Father Fitzgerald put the rehearsal off until tomorrow," Patrick said as they drew close. "Five o'clock. Be careful on the way down. It's ice all the way."

"Did you tell Molly?" Michael asked as Patrick started off again.

"I'll stop there on the way to school."

"Okay. Thanks. See you."

"Who was that?" Sam asked. "I've seen him around."

"Patrick O'Donnell. He's got the lead in the play we're doing this year." Michael pulled his scarf up around his mouth and hunched his shoulders against the cold.

Sam nodded. He didn't know any of the Irish kids well

except for Kathleen. He had always felt they were laughing at him and Pa when they walked around the square. "You and Pa love Charlestown for its history, for what it used to be," Michael had once told Sam. "I love it the way it is now. And Ma doesn't like it at all."

"Have you tried talking to Ma?" Sam asked as they stood waiting for the bus. "I wonder how it's going to be for her. What is she going to do?"

"I don't know," Michael said slowly. "All she's done for the last two years is take care of Pa, day in and day out. She was at that hospital every day he was sick from nine in the morning until nine at night. Now she's going to have a lot of empty time on her hands."

They were silent as two more people joined them at the stop.

"I don't know how she stood it," Michael said. "The hospital was so depressing with those sad, sick people and the dour-looking nurse they used to assign to Pa."

"Pa liked her. He said she was the best one in the hospital," Sam said. Michael had always avoided the hospital. He looked out of place and uncomfortable there, and Pa used to send him home. "He's too young to see me like this, Deborah. Don't let him come again." More excuses for Michael, Sam had thought. Sam always went, whenever his mother would let him. Except for once. Except for that last time.

The night before he died Pa went into a coma. "He isn't the same," Ma explained over the telephone the next morning. "He won't know you at all. He might not even see you."

"Then I'm not going," Sam cried, and for the first time in the two years of sickness he'd run away. When he came back to the house that afternoon, Pa had died. And Michael had been with him. Michael had seen him last.

Michael felt Sam's eyes on him again. "Is something

25

bugging you this morning?" he asked. "Why do you keep staring at me like that?"

"Why'd you go to the hospital that last time? When Pa was in the coma? You hated it so much."

Michael looked away. How queer, he thought, that we are standing outside in the cold talking about this. After all the silences between us in that empty house.

"I guess because it was the last time. I went to say good-bye."

"But Ma said he wouldn't know us," Sam cried. "How can you say good-bye to someone who can't even hear you?"

Michael looked down at his hands. He knew Sam wanted to know what Pa had looked like. Michael shuddered at the memory of his blank face. He knew now he'd never get that last picture of Pa out of his mind.

"Forget it, Sam," he muttered. He meant to say something more, to soften his words a little, but Sam turned away before he could speak again. Michael watched him go. Will it always be this way? he wondered. Will I always be so out of tune with the rest of the family? What's left of it.

One afternoon a couple of weeks later, Sam came home to find his mother sitting at the kitchen table. She looked up and smiled when he came in the room as if she had been waiting for him.

"Do you want something to drink?" she asked.

"I'll get it," he answered. He had avoided his mother in the weeks since Pa had died and he felt guilty about it. We should share what we're going through, he decided this afternoon on the way home from school. But it was hard to know where to start.

They sat across from each other in silence for a while.

"You look tired, Ma," he said.

26

She glanced up with her eyebrows lifted as if she were surprised that he'd noticed. "I am tired," she said quickly. "The bed seems so big. This whole house suddenly seems too big. Maybe we should go away for a while."

He didn't answer. She had been testing ideas out on them all week, and Sam found it hard to respond. He wanted to tell her to just relax and not do anything.

"I did some cleaning out today, Sam," she said, her voice a little brighter. "Come see."

He followed her down the hall to Pa's office. The room was empty. The books were gone from the shelves, the top of the desk was swept bare. He stared at the room in silence. He felt as if he'd suddenly come upon a great hole in the house.

"I'm going to use this room from now on," Ma said quickly. "I've always needed a place to work."

"But Ma, what about the empty room on the third floor? You've often talked about making that into a studio. If Michael and I fixed it up for you, you could start painting again."

"No, I need an office, a place to do my paperwork. This will be perfect," she said cheerily.

He stood looking out the corner window, down the hill. There was a terrible anger inside him that he was trying to contain. This had been Pa's place, the corner of the house where it was so easy to imagine him, tipped back in the chair, his long legs propped up on the desk. When he came home late from the hospital, he would stick his head in here first and check the mail or pull out a book. Sometimes Ma would have to come in and drag him away to eat his dinner, and he would arrive at the table still in his white coat that smelled of the hospital. Now she had swept it bare, taken away every trace of him.

"Well, what do you think, Sam?" she asked quietly.

"It just seems so soon, Ma—"

"This house is not going to be a memorial to your father," she snapped back at him. "I am only forty years old and I refuse to live in a tomb."

"Oh, I know that, Ma. You're right," he mumbled as he pushed past her. "It's probably for the best." After that, he went back to avoiding her rather than risk another argument.

In late April the first real signs of spring appeared. The streets down the hill were finally cleared of snow, and all that remained were the salt stains on the sidewalks. Sam walked up to the monument one day on his way home from school to look at the view. The ice in Boston Harbor had melted and from where he stood he could see a big tanker tying up. He walked home briskly, determined to drag Ma out of the dark house for a walk. She and Michael were sitting in the kitchen.

"It's beautiful out today," Sam said eagerly as he came in. "Why don't we all take a walk?"

Ma looked hesitant. "The dinner's on the stove."

"So turn it off for a while."

"Well, there was something I wanted to talk to you both about."

"Good," Michael said, jumping up. "We can talk about it outside. I'll get your coat." He was always happy to get out of the dark house.

They walked for a while in silence, around the monument and then down Adams Street toward the center of Charlestown.

"It is wonderful out today," Ma said. "It reminds me a little of early spring in Savannah. Except down there, the flowers are out by this time."

"What did you want to talk to us about, Ma?" Michael asked.

"I thought we might take a trip this summer. Take the

car and drive up through New England. I've been looking at the map, and I planned a route up through the White Mountains and then into western Maine and across the state."

"When would we be going?" Michael asked.

"The middle of June would be a good time," she said. "Before the big summer tourist rush."

"Do you think I could stay here, Ma? Father Fitzgerald has scheduled a lot of rehearsals for June."

Ma didn't say anything for a minute. She took a deep breath. "It's only for ten days, Michael," she said. "I thought it would be nice if we were all together. We are going to be here the whole summer, and that'll be hard after all those summers up at the Point."

"The play isn't that important, Michael," Sam burst out.

"It is to me," Michael said coldly. He glanced at Ma. "I'll see if Father Fitzgerald can move the rehearsals up earlier."

"Thank you, Michael," she said softly. He didn't answer.

At the next corner, they turned back up the hill toward home.

"We'll have a good time together," Ma said brightly, trying to fill the silence between them. "We can take our bathing suits and our rackets and have lots of picnics."

"Maybe we could stop at the Point," Sam said. "Just for a look at the old house."

"That might be fun," Ma said. "It will be hard for me not to just walk in and settle down for the summer." She stopped for a minute.

"I'll never forgive your father for selling that house out from under us," she said softly. "I would have done anything to keep it. I would have sold the house here first."

Sam nodded. Maybe Pa knew that, he thought.

Maybe he couldn't bear to know that we would all still have the Point after he had gone. He pushed the thought away.

"I'm going to drop in at the church," Michael said. "See you later."

Sam and Ma walked on up the hill together. "I seem to make Michael so angry these days," she said with a little smile. "Nothing I do is right."

"It's not just you," Sam said. "He's the same way with me."

When Michael came back that evening, Sam went into his room.

"Ma's got to work things out her own way," he said slowly. "I don't think you're giving her much support."

"But she's so boring. This must be at least the fifteenth plan this week." He shrugged. "She's trying to make us be a happy little family, and we're not."

"It's only ten days out of your precious life, Michael. Can't you even give that up?"

"And who are you, Sam? The official mourner? I said I'd go, didn't I? Now clear out of here and stop bugging me about it."

Sam left the room, slamming the door behind him.

The next afternoon, he waited on the corner to meet Kathleen on her way home from college.

"Boo," he said, jumping into her path.

"Hi, Sam." She smiled at him.

"Let's go down to the drugstore and have something to eat."

"Sure."

"How are you?" she asked as they walked down the hill.

"All right, I guess. We're all missing Pa, but nobody talks about it. We just seem to fight a lot. Ma spends her time rearranging the furniture and the pictures in the house as if she's trying to put her own stamp on it and erase any traces of Pa. Did I tell you she totally cleared out his office? The place is bare."

Kathleen nodded. "You did tell me that. But I can understand it. She has to make her own life now. Maybe this is her way of starting to do that. I never felt she was really at home in that house."

"Charlestown was always Pa's idea."

Kathleen smiled. "I remember that summer when he bought it. He would come out here every evening to see what the workmen had done. Peggy and I used to sit on the stoop and watch. You all must have been up in Maine."

"I didn't realize you were a stoop-sitter too," Sam said with a grin. Kathleen's younger sister, Peggy, was the neighborhood gossip. She could see most of the houses on their street from her perch on the Murphys' front stoop.

"There are lots of things you don't know about me, Sam Everett," Kathleen said. "Doesn't that sound mysterious?" she added, laughing at the expression on his face. They went into the drugstore and found a booth in the corner by the window. They ordered two Cokes and sat in silence for a minute, looking out the window.

"Do you think about him all the time?" Kathleen asked.

"I think about how everything is changing for me now," he answered slowly. "Now that he's gone I've begun to realize how he held us all together. He was the center of the wheel and the spokes aren't touching anymore." He felt his face turning red.

"The spokes?" she prodded.

"Me and Ma. Me and Michael." He paused. "Me and you," he said at last.

Kathleen looked out the window at the passing faces bundled up. The weather had turned cold again.

"You and Michael seem angry with each other these days," she said softly.

"We've never been close," Sam said. "We're different. Do you know he went to the hospital that last day? After Pa had gone into a coma."

"He told me," Kathleen said.

"It was the only time I didn't go," Sam whispered. "Why did he have to be there?"

Kathleen looked up at the sound of pain in his voice. "It doesn't really matter, Sam. Your father wouldn't have known if you were there or not."

"But *I* know," Sam said. "I know that I ran away the last day. I just couldn't stand to see him that way."

"I think you did the right thing," Kathleen said. She stood up and pulled on her coat. It was already dark out. "I've got to go. Mother will be wondering where I am."

"What do you mean, I did the right thing?"

"You still have the picture of your father as he was in your mind. Michael will probably never be able to forget the blank face he saw that last day."

"I'll walk back with you."

They walked close together, their heads bent against the wind. He walked her right to the door, but as usual she didn't ask him in. He had never been inside her house. Once when he asked if he could come in, she had said no. "I don't want you to see it. It's so different from yours. You'd be amazed."

"See you tomorrow?" he asked.

"I have a late class. Maybe the next day." She turned away quickly and went inside.

4

Peggy was sitting in the living room watching television when Kathleen walked through.

"Hanging out with Sam again?" she asked.

"None of your business," Kathleen said.

"Isn't he a little young for you?"

"Well, he's too old for you, so don't worry your little nosy head about it."

"You must like him or you wouldn't be acting so grouchy."

"What's up?" Kathleen asked, nodding toward the kitchen. She could hear her parents arguing with each other.

Peggy shrugged. "Nothing new. Daddy's yelling and Mum's just shaking her head. Our house gets more like a soap opera every day."

"The boys are out?"

Peggy laughed. "Are they ever in?"

Kathleen went up the stairs quietly. She didn't want her mother to call her into the kitchen. She had been in the middle of too many of their arguments lately.

Her desk was strewn with comic books. She piled them up and dumped them back on Peggy's bed.

She hated having to share a room with her sister. Nothing was sacred in a big family and especially with a little sister like Peggy. Kathleen sat down on her bed and looked around the room. The walls had never been repainted and after the leak in the roof last fall, the old paint was beginning to peel in long strips. She had put up a couple of big posters which made the room a little brighter but even they were curling away from the walls. The whole house looked like this. The furniture was old, and when something broke, it seemed to stay broken forever. When Kathleen complained to her mother, she just shrugged. "Some days I wonder how I'm going to feed all of you. Don't talk to me about furniture."

Kathleen arranged her books on the desk and sat down to do her homework. The window looked down on the street and if she pulled her chair in close to the desk, she could see the Everetts' house from here. She sat there for a long time watching the blank face of the house.

* * *

When Kathleen first pushed the door open and called up the stairway, there was no answer. Then Dr. Everett's head appeared over the banister.

"Sorry, I didn't mean to disturb you," she said. "I was looking for Sam."

"They're all out." They both hesitated a minute. She had not seen him in a while.

"Come on up," he said. "Sam just brought me an old book on colonial Charlestown architecture. It's one I've never seen before."

She still paused.

"Do you have to rush off somewhere?"

"No. I have some time."

"Come on up then. I haven't seen you in ages."

She threw her coat over the banister and climbed the stairs slowly. When she got to the top, she saw that he was in his bathrobe and slippers.

"Sorry about my informal dress," he said with a tinge of sarcasm in his voice. "I'm not really supposed to be out of bed yet."

"How are you feeling?" she asked as he led her into his office.

"I'm better now," he said slowly. "But this pneumonia was the worst ever. My blood seems to have turned to water," he added with a slight smile.

"Sam told me when you went into the hospital," Kathleen said.

"Why haven't I seen you around lately?" he asked gruffly. "I could have used the company."

"I didn't want to disturb you. And I've been down at the church with Father Fitzgerald a lot. We're working on a new play. The one Michael's in."

He nodded. "I've heard something about your rabble-rousing priest. From what I understand, he's got the whole neighborhood up in arms."

She didn't answer. They had argued once before about Father Fitzgerald.

"Look at these drawings. It's the first time I've ever seen a plan of the original town of Charlestown. This must have been done just before the British burned the place down, because we figured out that Ebenezer Whittlesey didn't move here until 1774, and there's the plan for his house."

"He was the doctor, wasn't he?"

"Right." He glanced at her. "I'd forgotten what a good memory you have."

She blushed at the compliment but he didn't notice. He was leafing through the book. She was horrified at how thin he looked. His face had grown old in the last few weeks.

"Here, sit down," he said, pulling over a chair for her. "I'm not very good at standing for long periods of time. I'm trying to find a description of the town and the main houses around the common."

He had always been this way with his books. The history of Charlestown is what had drawn him there in the first place.

He noticed her eyes on him, and he sat back in the chair. "I must look quite different," he said, running his hands through his hair.

"A little thinner," she said quietly. "But you've still got the energy for your books."

"I hope I don't ever lose that," he said. He turned back to the book. "Look, I've found the page I wanted to show you." She pulled her chair closer, and they sat hunched over the desk, poring over an old map that was followed by a description.

"This is the clearest plan we've ever seen of the original town," Kathleen said. "Where did Sam find this book?"

"He said something about ordering it from a bookstore in Beacon Hill." Dr. Everett smiled. "It was a nice present to come home to. Now look here, it shows the two churches across the common from each other. On either side there are the merchants' houses."

"The big shots in town," Kathleen said with a grin.

"But look, the plan shows a whole network of secondary streets with shops and smaller houses. The town was actually quite well developed when the British burned it down. I never realized that before." He leaned back in his seat and closed his eyes for a minute. "That small type gives me a headache."

36

Kathleen was still looking at the map. "It shows the location of Cotton Mather's house. Wasn't he the man with the huge library that was burned in the fire?"

"Yes, you're right." Dr. Everett opened his eyes but he did not lean forward again. He smiled at her. "Enough history for the moment. Now tell me, how are you? Did you finish the paper on Bunker Hill?"

"Yes. The teacher gave me an A. I brought back the books you lent me last week when you were still in the hospital."

"Are you going to let me read the paper?"

"If you want to," she said. "I'm working on something else now. A study of the Irish immigration to Charlestown from South Boston."

"Oh." He raised his eyebrows. He had never been very interested in the Irish history of Charlestown. "What got you started on that?"

"Father Fitzgerald suggested it. He had a book on the Irish in Boston, and it has a whole section on Charlestown in the late 1800s. You should read it," she said eagerly. He didn't answer. He sat in silence for a while, looking out the window. She thought he might have forgotten she was there.

"Did Sam tell you I sold the house in Maine?" he asked.

"Yes."

"I can't believe we will never see that old place again," he said softly.

"Mrs. Everett must have been very upset. I remember you telling me how much she loved it up there. When you came back in September, the car was usually piled high with the pictures she had painted."

"She always sat in this special corner of the front porch." He glanced down at his hands. "She was very angry with me. She loved that house more than any place except maybe the house she grew up in in Savannah."

"I remember the photograph Sam took of her painting on the porch."

"That was very good, wasn't it? I think it's the best thing he's ever done."

"That house had been in your family so long." She smiled. "Our family doesn't really have anything worth keeping."

"Yes. I suppose that Mother, wherever she is, must be furious with me. The house up at the Point was her favorite place in the world. She went there every single summer from June through September. I can still close my eyes and see her sitting in her favorite rocking chair on the porch or down walking over the rocks at low tide, picking mussels for dinner." He glanced at Kathleen. "Did you ever meet my mother?"

Kathleen shook her head. "Sam told me she wouldn't ever come to Charlestown."

He nodded.

"She must have hit the roof when you told her you were going to move here."

"Yes," he said with a smile. "She tried everything she could to stop me. She even threatened to write me out of her will, but it never came to that."

From downstairs, Kathleen could hear someone at the door. She stood up suddenly. She never felt very comfortable around Mrs. Everett. "I should go," she said.

He looked disappointed. "But I haven't found that description yet."

"I'm sorry. I promised my mother I would run some errands for her." She started to back out of the room.

"Come back again, Kathleen," he said. "You always cheer me up."

A shiver ran through her. "I will," she whispered. "I promise." She met Mrs. Everett on the steps.

"Hello, Kathleen. If you're looking for Sam, he's right behind me. He had to do an errand for me in town." She continued up the stairs without waiting for an answer. "Charles, I'm home."

Kathleen picked up her coat and slipped quietly out the door.

* * *

Just as she opened up her history book there came a knock on the bedroom door.

"Come in," she said reluctantly. Her mother slipped in quietly and shut the door behind her. Kathleen knew who it was without turning around.

"Yes, Mother?" she asked. "I was just starting to work."

Her mother sat down on the bed with a long sigh. "Your father's supervisor had a talk with him again today. One more late day, and he's going to fire him. Then what will we do?"

"Mother, you know why he's late. If he would stay in at night instead of drinking at the bar from five until two in the morning, he would be able to function like a normal human being." Kathleen saw again that picture of Dr. Everett, his blue eyes bright in the gaunt face. Then she thought of her father.

"They had to bring him home again last night. Tim McDougal said he passed out on the street right in front of the bar." Her mother stood up and straightened out the bedspread. "I don't know what to do anymore."

Kathleen swung around in her chair. "Mother, I told you about the group Father Fitzgerald runs down at the church for alcoholics. You should take Daddy to just one meeting and let him see what it's like."

Her mother frowned. "Your father is not an alcoholic, Kathleen, and I will not have you calling him that." Kathleen turned back to her desk. It seemed she and her mother kept on having the same arguments over and over again. "Anyway, your father will not go anywhere near that church after hearing the crazy ideas that priest has put in your head." Her mother went out of the room before Kathleen could answer.

Kathleen put her head down on the desk. This winter she felt more isolated than ever before. The kids she used to hang around with had dropped her completely when she'd started college in the fall. "They think you're just a snob like those Everett kids," Peggy told her. Her mother was alternately angry and weepy with her. "Why do you want to go to that college? What good will it do you? Why don't you just find a nice boy and settle down?" "Look where it got you, Mother," Kathleen had answered coldly. That time her mother had slapped her across the face and sent her up to her room.

Father Fitzgerald was the only one who knew what she went through every day. "It's worth it, Kathleen," he said. "The other kids are taunting you because they're jealous. They know that in the end you're going to be much freer." He smiled at her. "Just think of yourself as a kind of pioneer."

Now with Dr. Everett gone, she had no place to escape to where she could hide away from everybody. With him, she had always been able to lose herself.

She could hear Peggy coming up the stairs. She sat up and turned on the desk light.

5

The inn looked just like the picture on the brochure. White clapboard set back from a quiet road on a rolling green lawn, surrounded by thick old trees. It was the first night of their New England trip. They had driven up to New Hampshire through the White Mountains and down into Franconia. "The first night we're staying in a country inn," Ma had planned gaily. "After that it's all motels."

Sam stood out on the porch among the empty wicker chairs. "Our season hasn't really started yet," the woman at the front desk had explained. He loved the deep June greens and the high dark trees, the sweet and tickling smell of new-mown grass, the black country road that turned and dipped down into the town. Standing on the porch, he felt a pull inside, a longing for the time he would decide where to live. Now that Pa was gone, Charlestown didn't have to be home anymore. It was Pa's love and dedication to the place that had kept them all there. But he was sure they'd stay at least for a while.

Ma seemed too tired and confused to change even the smallest part of her life.

She came out and stood beside him. "It's pretty, isn't it?" she asked. He nodded, wishing she wouldn't talk. The best part of it was the silence. She sat down in a wicker chair and listened with him.

The next day they took the road up along the Androscoggin River through Errol, where the logs came bumping down the river to the pulp mill, then east across the border into Maine along the Rangely Lakes, where the pine trees grew thick and dark down to the water, and the towns were small and scattered and empty.

"I wouldn't want to be stuck up here in the winter," Michael said. "You might as well be in Antarctica."

"It's different from the coast," Sam said. "So dark and empty. I miss the fishing towns with the white houses and the boats and the crowded sidewalks."

"They are just as deserted in the winter," Ma said. "You remember those trips up to get the Christmas tree? Even Boothbay looked like a morgue."

"Are we going to go by the house?" Sam asked quietly.

"Sure," Ma said brightly. "Why not?"

"Lots of reasons," Michael muttered from where he was stretched out in the back seat. "You and Sam will get all sad and grouchy and from the Point down to Charlestown, it will be the same old September trip. Clouds of gloom."

"You hated to leave it just as much as the rest of us," Sam said.

"Maybe. I just was better at seeing the bright side of life," said Michael wryly.

"He's right," Ma said gently. "It will make us sad."

"I still want to go," Sam said. "You can drop me off at the end of the road and I'll walk down."

"No," said Ma. "If we get that far, I want to go in, too."

They found a motel very late that night. The sign said NO VACANCY, but Ma decided to try it anyway.

"I'm too tired to drive any farther," she muttered.

The place looked dingy from the outside but the inside was worse. The lobby smelled of sweet disinfectant, and there were flies everywhere. The boy at the desk stared at them sullenly.

"Do you have two rooms?" Ma asked.

"Didn't you see the sign?"

"I thought maybe—" Her voice drifted off. "We've driven awfully far today and we're tired."

The boy just shrugged.

"Where's the nearest motel?" Michael asked.

"About twenty miles down. In Anson."

"Do you have a bathroom I could use?" Ma asked.

"Customers only," the boy said as he turned away.

When they got back to the car, Ma's head began to jerk. It was a funny backward twitch she got when she was nervous. Sam hadn't noticed her doing it in a long time. He hated it.

"We should have brought some camping gear," Michael said as he slammed the door.

"It certainly would help if one of you could drive," Ma barked.

Neither of them answered her. There was nothing they could say.

The next place had two small rooms. Ma signed for them.

"I like the naked light bulb," Michael said jauntily. "Just the right touch."

Sam bounced up and down on the mattress. "Thin but serviceable," he remarked. They were talking a little falsely to cover up their nervousness. Ma's mood was changing and they both could sense it. They knew the signs so well from times before.

Those were the times that she acted strangely, out of tune with herself. She giggled when nothing was funny and flirted with the two of them like a girl friend. Her face was made up and her voice was loud and she used words like "bitch" and "ass," coarse words that made Sam shake with anger. The whole house felt different. His father never came home until late, and when he came his eyes looked wary and restless. "Is your mother home?" was always his first sharp question, and if Sam or Michael said no, he would relax a little. But if Ma was in her room, he'd walk quietly up the stairs with his shoulders sagging, like a little boy going up for his punishment. And from below, the boys could hear the calm, steady voice of their father cutting through the eerie laughs and the shouts, as if he were repeating the same thing over and over. Something was wrong with her but they never talked about it. Pa avoided the question in Sam's eyes.

"She has sort of spells," Sam tried to explain to Kathleen. "Strange vague times when she wanders around the house in a robe and smiles all the time for no reason, and her face looks gray and closed up."

"Maybe she's a schizophrenic," Kathleen offered. "I've read about them. One mood one day and the opposite mood the next. They're on a kind of seesaw."

Sam shook his head. "It's not like that. She's just vague and messy and sad and unpredictable. And the moods always start with this jerking of her head. A twitch she gets. Then you know there's a bad time coming on."

The spells had stopped when Pa got sick. Then she had been efficient and cheerful, and when she was sad, it was "normal" sad. And when she was irritated, the anger came out directly, instead of in that strange high laugh and the false polite voice.

The walls between their rooms were thin and the boys could hear Ma talking to herself. The same words over and over again like a strange chant.

"What's she doing?" Sam finally asked.

Michael shrugged. "Saying her prayers, I guess. I don't know." He wiggled his bare toes at the end of the bed. "It looks like that funny mood is coming on again."

"I really hate her when she's like that," Sam said. "It makes me feel she's a hundred miles away and too close at the same time."

"You shouldn't let it get to you so much. Just clear out of the house," Michael said.

"That's always been your answer," Sam said quietly. He was remembering those days Pa had been in the hospital and Michael had never been with them. Michael glanced at Sam without saying anything. This mood that Ma was getting in worried him too, although he and Sam had never talked about it. He felt sorry for her more than angry. Those days she seemed like a lost, lonely child, too scared to reach out to any of them for help. When she was in that mood they all closed down into their separate selves.

Late that night, Sam woke up. He stared out the window for a long time, watching the neon sign across the street flash RESTAURANT/BAR on and off. Next door, Ma was still up. He could hear her moving about in her room. After a while, he heard her front door open and close and then silence. He thought of waking Michael and going after her, but he was sure Michael would laugh at him. "Oh, let her alone," Michael would say. "You're not her guardian angel." So Sam turned over and went back to sleep.

They met for breakfast in the coffee shop. Ma looked tired and drawn, but she acted as if nothing was wrong.

"I thought we'd drive straight for the coast today without stopping," she said. "Backwoods Maine is beginning to depress me."

"I agree," Michael said. "The natives aren't very friendly."

Ma poured herself another cup of coffee. Her hand was shaking. Sam watched the stream of black liquid vibrate into the cup.

"How did you sleep, Ma?" he asked quietly.

"Not very well. You boys will have to keep me awake on the road today."

She drove very fast, as if they were in a hurry to get somewhere else, to leave something behind. She seemed distracted, so they talked very little. They all knew they were going to the Point to look at the house.

They drove through the town in the late afternoon. The summer season had not started yet, and the streets seemed oddly deserted and quiet. Sam watched the familiar stores crawl by—the drugstore where the gum machine jammed and the movie theater that closed down every Labor Day and the grocery store with the bingo announcement that had faded in the sun. Then the road curved around past the town dock. In late summer the water was dotted with sailboats, but this afternoon the fishing boats were the only ones unloading at the dock.

"It hasn't changed at all, has it?" Michael said in an oddly quiet voice.

"I guess it never will," Sam said. He was already feeling a strange mixture of dread and excitement as they turned off the main street on the road to the Point.

6

The car rounded the last turn and the house stood up before them. Its whiteness struck Sam first: the straight, bone-white clapboard line punctured here and there by the blue shutters and the empty dark windows. It waited there all year for them to come back and open the doors and put out the porch chairs and paint the railings. Sam remembered the smells in the house: the old wood of the pine floors, the salty sour smell of kelp that rose from the ocean, the oil paints from Ma's corner of the porch, and always the smell of the pine woods that crowded down to the shore.

All of this came to him now as they stood beside the car and stared at the house. Suddenly he wished they hadn't come. Seeing the place like this only brought back the happier times when they had all been there together.

* * *

"Sam, will you come for a sail with me after lunch?" Pa asked. They were eating on the porch the way they often did in the summer. Pa leaned across the table and quietly picked a crust of bread off Ma's plate. She smiled at him. She never ate her crusts. "The wind is out of the southwest. We could beat it out to the Egg Islands and have a clear sail back in time for dinner."

"Sure, Pa. I'd like that."

"How about you, Michael?"

"No, thanks, Pa. I have a rehearsal scheduled for three o'clock in the shed," Michael said. His group, the Point Players, were putting on two of Chekhov's one-act plays that summer.

"You work that group hard, don't you?" Pa asked with a smile. "I'm surprised you haven't had a rebellion yet."

Michael shrugged. "I'm pretty careful with the schedule. I never plan a rehearsal when there's a sailing race or a tennis match. Our first show is just two weeks from today."

"How's it going?" Ma asked.

"All right, but we haven't done anything about the set for the first play." Michael glanced at her. "I was hoping you would help us design something."

"Me?" Ma asked. "I'm flattered, Michael, but I've never done set design before. I don't think I'd be very good at it. I work on such a small scale with the canvas."

"We don't need anything elaborate. The action all takes place in Madame Popova's drawing room. If you could just do a backdrop that suggested the outlines of the room, then we could use tables and chairs to fill it in." They were all silent for a moment. Ma seemed to be thinking.

"I could get you the wood from the lumberyard, Deborah," Pa said. "Try planning it out first on a piece of paper."

"All right," she said with a smile. "I'll try. But I'm not promising anything." She began to stack the plates.

"I guess that takes care of you for the afternoon," Pa said with a frown. "I was going to ask if you wanted to come for a sail with us."

"Sorry, Charles. Maybe tomorrow."

"Your mother can always find an excuse not to sail," Pa said to Sam, as they followed her inside with another pile of plates. It was Sam's turn to do the dishes. "I'm going to weed the patch of flowers by the front steps," Pa said. "I'll meet you down at the boat in a little while."

When Sam was finished in the kitchen, he came back out on the porch. Ma was sitting at the edge of the big wicker chair in front of her easel, dabbing her brush first at the paint, then at the canvas. Sam came up quietly and stood behind her, watching as her head and shoulders moved back and forth, considering the picture from different angles. She was wearing a wide-brimmed straw hat to keep the sun off her face and when she turned around to see who was standing there, its floppy frame made her look young and soft. She looked so pretty, her cheeks two high spots of red and her eyes almost black.

"Do you like the picture?" she asked.

He considered it for a long time. "I think it's the best of your landscapes," he said slowly. "But the sketch you did of Pa will always be my favorite picture."

"You'd better go on," she said. "Pa went down to the boat quite a while ago."

"Bye, Ma," he said, leaning over quickly to give her a kiss on the cheek. "See you later."

*   *   *

This time Michael was the first to move. He left them standing by the car and walked up to peer into the living room windows. The sight of him looking into their house made Sam shiver. He glanced at Ma. She stood and stared as if she were in a trance.

"Come on," Michael called. "The furniture's all covered up. There's nobody here yet."

It was funny the way they scattered, each to a favorite place. Ma went up and settled herself in a corner of the porch to watch the sea.

Michael and Sam went back to look at the shed. There was a small room behind the stage that had been turned into a darkroom for Sam the summer after he took the photography course. He laughed now when he remembered his first pictures. "Gull Soaring over Black Rocks" and "Two Trees in Shadow." But there had been one good picture. He had snuck up behind Ma and snapped her profile as she stared out over her easel at the ocean. The light was just right so that it caught the dips and edges of her face, the high forehead, the long eyelashes and the short curved nose, the upward turn of her upper lip and her small bump of a chin. The pieces in between were all sunk in the shadows so that it was not a photograph of a specific person but more an idea of someone. Pa loved the picture. Sam blew it up for him, and he hung it beside his bureau at home. Ma never said anything much to Sam about it, but he found her once or twice staring at it intently.

The shed was locked so they wiped circles in the dirty windows to look through.

"The stage is still there," Michael said in a hushed voice. "I wonder if they use it."

Suddenly, Sam had an urge to shout. "Hello," he cried at the dusty rooms. Michael glanced at him. "I feel as if we're at a funeral," Sam said sheepishly. "All over again." Then he turned away quickly because he was scared something was going to explode inside him.

"Do you want to look at the house?" Michael asked.

Sam shook his head and turned down the path to the

water. He didn't want to look inside a house that no longer belonged to them, at rooms where the furniture and the paintings were different. He wanted to remember the house the way he had known it. It was the same thing with Pa. Sam wanted to remember him the way he had known him.

Michael came up beside him, and they stood together silently, looking out over the dull gray water. The sky had turned cloudy, and the leaden color was reflected in the ocean.

"If you swim far enough, you'll hit Spain," Michael said quietly. Sam smiled at the old joke.

"This is it, I. guess," Sam said, looking back at the house. "We'll never see it again."

"I know," Michael answered. "But there'll be other places for us. Other special houses."

"Not like this one."

Michael didn't answer. He knew what Sam meant.

Ma called to them from the porch and pointed to the car. The three of them walked over and got in without saying anything. Ma backed out the driveway, and Sam looked back to see the house framed by the low-hanging branches of the corner pine tree. And then it was gone.

"Good-bye," Ma said awkwardly into the silence. That was all anybody said for a long time.

They drove until darkness and stopped in another motel. Ma didn't seem to notice they had missed dinner. She said goodnight quickly and shut her door. Sam and Michael ate in a diner next door.

"We're going home tomorrow," Michael said. "She told me while you were paying the man for the gas."

"I'm not surprised," Sam said. "Seeing the house made this whole trip seem—" He stopped and thought. "Sort of false, I guess."

"What do you mean?"

"As if we're trying to make a new life for ourselves before any of us is ready."

Michael nodded. He felt sorry for Sam. Michael had something to look forward to in Charlestown, while Sam had nothing. His whole life had revolved around Pa's sickness in the last year.

"You should go back to your photography," Michael said. "Your darkroom upstairs is still set up, isn't it?"

Sam nodded. He hadn't looked at his camera for a year and his eyes no longer framed pictures the way they used to. I can't just pick up my life and go on as if nothing has happened, he thought. I need to spend some time just thinking and remembering. Some time to mourn.

The accident happened late the next day just outside Boston. Ma had not said a word all afternoon, and her face looked tight and drawn. Sam noticed that she was driving vaguely, changing lanes without using the blinker, speeding up suddenly and then slowing down too quickly. He watched her face for signs of that old tension but her head was not twitching and she did not talk at all. Her eyes had a driven look as if she were impatient to get somewhere fast.

The accident was a small one. Sam saw it coming, and he cried out but it was too late. She changed lanes without looking carefully and their car clipped the one coming up behind them. There was a jolt and a strange crunch as their bumpers bent, and then the cars parted again. Ma slowed down but did not stop.

"Ma, what are you doing? You have to pull over," Sam shouted.

The other driver drew up beside them and pointed angrily to the side of the road. Ma did not look at him or at Sam. She just kept staring down the road as if she were connected to it, and there was no way to get off. Michael leaned over the back of the seat and spoke very quietly in her ear.

"Ma, put on the blinker and pull over slowly. You have to do it now. Over to the right. Very slowly. That's right."

To Sam's surprise, she was obeying him like a robot finally under control. The car bounced onto the shoulder and drew slowly to a stop. Michael leaned over and took out the ignition key.

He handed Sam her wallet. "Go talk to him," he said quietly. "Explain that she's not well. I'll stay here with Ma."

The man was very angry, but Sam managed to keep him away from their car. They exchanged names and addresses and examined the damage, which was slight.

"You kids were lucky," the man said. "We could all be dead right now." He got back in his car. "I'll be in touch with your mother."

When Sam got back to the car, Ma was sitting in the back seat. She looked as if she'd been crying. Sam looked over at Michael.

"What did he say?" Michael asked.

"He'll be calling us in the next few days. He was mad." Sam shrugged. "How do you feel, Ma?" he asked gently.

"I'm very tired. I can't drive anymore." Her voice sounded whiny and her fingers picked nervously at her pocketbook.

"Well, we can wait," Sam said. "You could lie down in the back seat and try to sleep."

Ma shook her head.

"She wants you to drive," Michael said.

"I can't," Sam said. "I don't have a license."

"You've driven this car up at the Point."

"But that was on the dirt roads, Michael. This is the highway." Sam was pleading now, knowing he was going to have to do it.

"You can drive as slowly as you want. I'll watch the signs and tell you exactly where to go."

He slid over into the driver's seat. Michael handed him the key, and he started the car.

The drive home seemed to take hours although it was only forty minutes. Sam drove in the right lane the whole time while Michael talked to him in the same calm voice he had used to control his mother. It was a voice Sam had never heard before.

"All right, up here you have to go down the exit ramp where that green car is going. That's right. Now keep to the left so you get on the road for the tunnel."

"Why is that man honking?"

"You forgot to use the blinker."

"Damn."

"It's all right. He had plenty of room. Now we stay on this for a while."

The whole way home Ma was silent. Sam caught sight of her face a couple of times in the rearview mirror. She seemed oblivious to what was happening to them. He guided the car very slowly through the narrow streets of Charlestown and pulled it up in front of their house.

"We made it," Michael said.

Sam grinned at him. "Boy, you sound relieved. I didn't realize you were so worried."

"Ma, we're home," Michael said to the dark silence in the back seat.

She nodded. Slowly they got out of the car. Michael took her up to her room while Sam brought in the suitcases. The high, narrow front hall seemed darker than ever, and the house smelled closed up and musty, the way it always had when they first opened the door in

September. He stood at the bottom of the stairs and looked up toward the light of the second floor. He had stood here before on that dark cold day when he came home to find the house empty. He had known even before they told him that Pa was dead.

Michael appeared at the top of the stairs and waved at Sam to come up. They carried their suitcases to the third floor and sat down in Michael's room.

"What's she doing?" Sam asked.

"She said she was tired. She doesn't want us to get her up for dinner."

"What's wrong with her?" Sam asked.

"I don't know. I don't think it's just being tired."

Michael opened his record player and flipped down the record without looking at it. Sam picked up his suitcase and went down the hall into his room. He opened the window and leaned out. The kids were sitting on the monument steps as usual. Over at Kathleen's house the windows were pushed open, but he couldn't see anybody. Kathleen was baby-sitting for a family in Cape Cod. She wouldn't be back for ten more days. Down below in his mother's room, he could hear doors opening and closing. Then there was silence.

7

Ma did not come out of her room the next day. Sam and Michael knocked and called to her to come eat, but the door was locked and her muffled voice from inside the room told them to go away.

"We've got to do something," Sam said desperately when the second day had passed and they hadn't seen her.

"What do you want to do?" Michael muttered. "We can't break down the door."

"What is she doing in there?"

"Grieving," Michael said simply. "Do you want more milk?"

Sam shook his head. "There are noises coming from the room. Sometimes in the middle of the night. And she's talking to herself." He looked out the window. "It's so strange."

Michael stared at him without saying anything.

"Well, don't you think so?" Sam asked.

"I think you're strange," Michael said. "You should

get out of here. Forget about it for a while. Go back to your photography. You've spent the last two years living and dying with Pa. You've got to start living your own life again."

"Don't you care at all what happens to anybody but yourself?" asked Sam, his voice shaking with anger.

"And what good do you think it does to tiptoe around the house and listen to the strange noises in Ma's room?" Michael asked. "If you're not going to get an ax and break down the door, you might as well go out and forget about it. That's what I plan to do. I'll be down at the church if you want me." He ran some water over the dishes in the sink and left the room.

It was a cool morning. Michael walked down the hill slowly. He was glad to be back in Charlestown and glad to be out of the house. He didn't know what was wrong with Ma but he wanted to get away from her and think about something else.

The door to the auditorium was unlocked. Father Fitzgerald was in his office. He waved at Michael.

"How was your vacation?" he asked.

"Not much of a vacation." Michael shrugged. "About what I expected."

"How is your mother doing?"

"Not very well. In the beginning she had all sorts of plans. She was going to sell the house and then she was going to redecorate and then we were going to move to Beacon Hill and then nothing at all happened. The trip was another of those plans, and she hadn't really thought it out very well." Michael sat down on the edge of the desk. "We ended up going back to look at the old house and that pretty much did us in."

"The house in Maine?"

"Yes. Pa sold it last year without telling Ma. She was

furious when she found out. The house had been in Pa's family for a long time. We'd been going up there every summer." Michael paused. "He loved that place."

"It must have been hard for him to sell it," the priest said quietly.

"It was."

Father Fitzgerald leaned back in his chair. "You've got to give your mother some time. She'll go through different stages."

"Now she's taken to her bedroom. Sam and I haven't seen her since we got back Monday night. She must come out at night to get something to eat."

Father Fitzgerald frowned. "That does sound a bit extreme."

"What's going on around here? How have the rehearsals been going?"

"Up and down. Patrick has missed quite a few. I don't think he likes this play much."

"I'm always here if he drops out." Michael smiled. He was the understudy for Patrick's part, and more than once he had had to act it in the rehearsals. "Have you done anything about props?"

"No. I haven't concentrated on that. I suppose we should."

"I was thinking Sam might be able to help out. He's a good carpenter, and right now, he's just sitting up in the house moping around." The idea had occurred to Michael walking down the hill. He wasn't sure what Sam's reaction would be.

"Why don't you ask him," the priest said as he stood up. "We can always use more free help around here."

But Sam wasn't interested. The drama group was Michael's territory and he didn't want to compete.

"It would get you out of the house," Michael said.

"No, thanks. I don't need to get out of the house."
Michael didn't mention it again.

Sam began to enjoy the emptiness and freedom of the
house and he spent the days wandering through the
rooms, looking at the books and touching the pieces of
furniture that his father worried over and repaired and
moved from room to room to find just the right place.

He spent most of his time in the empty room on the
third floor. The space had never been refinished. Great
chunks of plaster had fallen off the wall, and strips of old
flowered wallpaper curled down from the slanted eaves.
The dormer window looked out over the roofs toward
Boston and on a clear day you could see the sun
sparkling on the water in the harbor. This was the room
that Pa had talked about turning into a studio for Ma,
but somehow he'd never gotten around to it.

When they were younger, Sam and Michael had
played here after school. Now the room held the
family's leavings—the children's books and broken toys
and suitcases and Sam's old bike. There was a peculiar
smell that someone finally pinned down to the gerbils
that had died there one winter when the heat went off.
Sam and Michael used to pick through the piles like
archaeologists through relics, taking some bent tin toy
back to their room to be cleaned up and used again.
Kathleen also used to explore in that room. "Why, the
whole history of your family is sitting right here," she
said the day she found the scrapbooks. There was an old
filing cabinet stuck behind a trunk in one corner, and the
drawers of it were stuffed with pictures and articles and
old letters. Sam had meant to ask Pa about the people in
the pictures, but then Pa had gotten sick and Sam had
forgotten about them.

So now when his mother stayed in her room and

Michael went down to the church after breakfast every morning, Sam climbed the stairs to the third floor and pored over the history of his family. He stared at the people in the brown curling photographs, trying to find in the younger, smoother features the faces of his grandparents and his aunts and uncles. Sometimes the pictures were labeled: "Theodore after his fishing trip in New Hampshire." "Holly with her friend Agatha from school." "Charles sitting in his Uncle John's new Model T." Pa's face was thin and unlined, and his dark hair sat over his high forehead like a bush. He had a wide loose smile that made him look younger than he was. Michael had that same look, Sam thought, whenever he laughed unexpectedly.

Then slowly they began to creep into the pictures. Sam as a baby in his grandfather's arms. Sam could only vaguely remember his grandfather: a tall, severe man with a sharp voice. His hair was full and white, and Sam remembered reaching out and pulling it once when he was being given a pony ride on the bony, gray-flanneled knee. He had been snatched away by his mother. "Oh, no, Sam, you mustn't pull Gramp's hair." But his grandfather had only laughed. "It's all right, Deborah. I like a brave boy." But Sam hadn't felt brave. Only curious.

There was another picture of the whole family assembled after Thanksgiving lunch on Beacon Hill. The faces looked stiff and composed, and Theodore was missing because he had taken the picture. Sam peered at himself standing stiffly beside his mother, dressed in wool shorts and long socks. Michael was perched on his father's shoulders. Ma looked nervous and was sitting up very straight, the way she always did for pictures.

Ma was always fussing over them when they went to the big, dark Beacon Hill house for Sunday lunch. Aunt

Holly and Uncle Theodore were there too, she in a wide black hat and he tall and loud, talking about guns and fishing and law. And Aunt Lydia, thin and straight in the corner, staring fiercely out at the children. She had never married, and as time went by, she came less and less to the family lunches.

Aunt Holly's children were older and everybody called them "the girls." Sarah and Kate always sat on either side of their grandmother and crossed their feet together and begged to hold Michael, even when he was too old to be "held." Reluctantly, Ma would sit him down in their laps, but the moment he started to squirm, she would snatch him back again.

"He won't break, Deborah," Grandma would say in her loud, commanding voice. "You mustn't fuss over him so."

"Yes, Mother," Ma would say, blushing and letting her son down to the floor. The minute he was released, Michael rushed around the room, playing tag with himself, knocking the antique chairs and making the china cups jiggle and clink in their saucers. "But that's why I hold on to him," Ma tried to explain to her mother-in-law when a chair did finally fall over. "He's so restless."

"But you must learn to control him with your voice, not your hands," Grandma answered. "Michael, come here and sit down." Her voice blared out across the conversations in the room. Everybody stopped talking and looked at Michael, who was playing with a backgammon set. He didn't move.

"Michael," the voice blared again.

"Michael," said Ma, starting toward him.

"Deborah, leave him alone. He must learn to listen," Grandma said sharply.

Finally, he looked up. "Come here and sit down by

me," Grandma said, patting the pillow on the velvet couch. Without a word, Michael jumped up and bolted out of the room.

"Good heavens," said Grandma with a little smile. "I didn't know I was *that* horrid."

Everybody laughed and started to talk again, relieved that the silence was over.

One day as Sam sat there, there was a voice behind him. "What are you doing?"

He jumped and turned guiltily.

"I was looking at the scrapbooks," Sam said.

"Why?" Ma asked from the doorway of the room. She was dressed in an old bathrobe of Pa's, and although she had obviously tried to pull herself together, her face looked wasted. Empty and white and lifeless. The old tense times were back.

Sam didn't answer her question. "Are there any pictures of your family?" he asked.

"There's one book in there somewhere. Buried under the mountains of Everett memorabilia." Her voice was tinged with a sharp sarcasm that Sam had not heard before.

He turned back to the book that was open in his lap. "Do you know who these people are, Ma?" he asked. If I can only get her out of the room for a while, he thought. She looked at him without answering. After a while, she came in and stood behind him, looking down at the book he was holding. The pictures were of people he did not know, tall ladies in hats and long dresses, standing about on the wide stone porch of a large house.

"Do you know who they are?" Sam repeated, shifting his position so she could see.

She stared at the pictures for a long time. "I'm not sure," she said, jerking her head back with that awful twitch. "Probably some ghastly cousins of your grandmother's." She started out of the room, and Sam scrambled to his feet to follow her.

"Do you want something to eat, Ma? We have some hamburger in the icebox. We've been using the money that was left over in the coffee can." Soon after Pa had gotten sick, Ma had started leaving the boys money to buy food for their dinner on the days she stayed late at the hospital.

She went down the stairs to the kitchen without answering him. He followed her quietly and stood in the door watching her. When she saw him, she frowned. "Where's Michael?" she asked.

"Down at the church," Sam said. "Where else?"

"What the hell does he do down there all day," she muttered. "That priest must be trying to convert him or something."

Sam felt a strange stab of loyalty for his brother. "They're putting on a play in August. Michael's got one of the big parts."

She nodded vaguely as if she hadn't heard. He knew she wanted him to go away and stop watching her, but he didn't want to make things that easy for her.

"Don't you have something else to do?" she asked.

"We've been worried about you, Ma," he said hesitantly. "Ever since we came home from the trip, you've been in your room. You have to take care of yourself," he ended lamely. He wanted to say, What the hell have you been doing?

"You sound just like your father," she said in a tired voice. "I take care of myself in my own way." She picked the wet sponge out of the sink and wiped up some sugar that had spilled on the table. Her hands were shaking and she moved jerkily, like someone who has been sick for a long time. Some of the sugar spilled onto the floor but she didn't lean down to sweep it up.

"Don't you want some lunch?" he asked, as she sat down with a cup of coffee.

"Sam, do me a favor," she said in a low voice. "Please just get the hell out of here and leave me alone."

The words were so sharp and rude that they stunned him. He went slowly up to his room and slammed the door.

"Goddamn bitch," he muttered to himself, pronouncing with careful pleasure words he had never used before.

8

Kathleen came home soon after that. Sam was out when she first arrived. He found a note taped to the door. "I'm home. Nobody answered the door. Call me when you get back." He glanced down the street at the Murphy house. Peggy was hanging out the window. He waved to her, and she ducked her head inside. He went down to wait for Kathleen on the front steps of his house and it wasn't long before she joined him.

"Peggy saw you come home," Kathleen said as she sat down beside him.

"Peggy sees all," he said with a grin. She smiled back. Her thin face had gotten tan, and there was a little trail of freckles across the top of her nose.

"What are you staring at?" she asked, touching her face.

"Your freckles," he said. "They're new."

She blushed. "I was out in the sun a lot. That's what always happens to my poor nose in the summer."

"I like them," he said. There was a silence between them. "How was the job?" he asked at last.

"Well, it wasn't a vacation. I had to take care of three

kids from breakfasttime until they went to bed. And for that, I got paid forty dollars a week. Slave labor." She shrugged. "The place was pretty nice. The house was right on the beach." She was trying to sound nonchalant because she knew he was used to places like that. She had seen pictures of their house in Maine. But she had never been to a beach before where there were long stretches of empty clean sand and water and an occasional bird skimming the tops of the waves. Even though she'd stayed there for three weeks, she'd never gotten used to the space and the silence and the sharp brightness of the sun on the water. In the mornings she'd get up before the children and tiptoe across the lawn wet with dew onto the cold sand rippled by the tide's markings.

"How was your trip?" she asked. "Peggy said you came back early."

Up above them a window scraped open in Ma's room. Sam motioned to Kathleen. They went inside and walked quietly up to the third floor. They sat down at either end of the wide window ledge and pulled up their knees.

"Is she sleeping?" Kathleen asked, pointing downstairs.

Sam shrugged. "She's been in there ever since we got back from the trip ten days ago. I've only seen her once. Michael is down at the church all day with Father Fitzgerald. They're working on a new play."

"I know. He told me about it before you left."

"So, anyway, he's no help. He keeps telling me to get out of the house," Sam said.

"Doesn't she come out for dinner or anything?"

"No, there was only one time. She looked terrible and she acted very strange. She was angry and rude with me for no reason."

"Maybe it has finally hit her that he died, and he's

never coming back again. A sort of delayed reaction. Maybe she's just hiding for a while from life." Kathleen looked at him. He was struck once more by the gray-green color of her eyes.

"I don't even believe it yet," Sam said quietly. "I wonder if I ever will."

They were silent for a while. Sam shook off a shiver and spoke again.

"There's something else. There is something wrong. It's been wrong for a long time. You know those funny moods that she has from time to time."

Kathleen looked out the window, her face tight.

"Well, that's the way she is. Vague and rude and distant, as if her mind is always somewhere else. And she can't function at all. We had a car accident on the way home. It wasn't too bad but she got in the back seat and wouldn't move. I had to drive the rest of the way."

"You don't have a license," Kathleen said.

"There wasn't anybody else."

She looked at him with what Sam liked to think was respect. They were silent again. Through the open windows came the voices of children shouting to each other around the monument. A truck strained its way up Winthrop Street and shifted gears just below them. Suddenly Sam closed his eyes and saw the porch up at the point. Low gray clouds hung over the horizon the way they used to before it rained. He could smell the clean spruce trees and the sea spray and the mown grass. The ache inside of him was sharp for the loss of the things Pa took with him when he went.

"I know what's wrong with your mother, Sam," Kathleen said quietly. Her tone of voice brought him back again, and he opened his eyes. She does know, he realized. She has known for a long time.

"Your mother's an alcoholic. She drinks. Right now she is probably sitting in her bed with a bottle between her knees." She began to talk more quickly as she watched the anger and fear rise up his face into his eyes. "I know all about it, Sam. My father is an alcoholic, too. He always has been. He goes down to the bar with the other men, and they drink and joke and pick fights, and he comes home, wild and angry, and Mother keeps him away from the younger kids. Your mother does it all in secret. She has been drinking for years. Your father told me."

"It's not true," Sam said coldly. "You're lying. You never did like Ma."

"Listen to me, Sam—"

"Shut up. You don't know anything. If it were true, Pa would have told me, not you. He wasn't your father."

"I dragged it out of him, Sam. He didn't really want to tell me but I came out and asked him once when I saw the strange way she was acting."

"Get out," Sam spat. "I don't want to talk to you about it." He turned away from the hurt look in her face.

"You'll have to talk to someone about it, Sam. Don't just try to hide it like your father did. That didn't work."

"Don't talk about him," Sam shouted. "Don't ever talk about him to me again."

She didn't move. Sam knew she was right. He had accepted what she said the moment she said the words. But he wasn't even thinking about his mother yet. He was thinking about his father and Kathleen, about the relationship they must have had without him. He was feeling betrayed by both of them.

"I'll see you, Sam," she said softly as she stood up. She hesitated for a minute as if she were hoping he would say something more, but he was silent. He heard the stair-boards creak as she went down.

Sam was sitting at the kitchen table when Michael came home.

"What's for dinner?" Michael asked, pulling open the door of the refrigerator.

"I didn't go to the store today," Sam said.

"I forgot, too. Do you have any money?" he asked. "I have about five dollars."

Sam found his wallet and opened it. "Three," he said. "And some change. The money in the coffee can has run out."

"All right. Let's go out. We could go over to that sausage restaurant. In the North End." Michael laughed. "The one Pa used to take us to when Ma disappeared into her bedroom. It seems about time we abandoned ship."

Sam looked hesitant. "Come on," Michael said, drumming out a beat on the table. "You look terrible, and I've got too much energy to slouch around in this depressing place."

"All right," Sam said. "I've got something to tell you anyway."

The place was crowded but they found a small table next to an old couple who were arguing loudly in Italian.

"Just like home," Michael said to Sam with a smile.

Sam smiled back at the old joke. Michael was always complaining that their house was too quiet. He'd come slamming up the stairs, singing and beating his books against the banister rail. "Anything to give the place a little life," he used to say.

"You said you had something to tell me?" Michael asked, turning away from the noisy room to look at his brother.

Sam looked down at his hands. "I know what's wrong with Ma," he said.

"Don't keep me in suspense," Michael said.

"She drinks. She's an alcoholic."

"What do you mean? She's never had a drop to drink in her life."

"Not in front of us. She drinks in her room. I guess she goes on binges from time to time, and this is one of them."

"How do you know?"

"Kathleen told me," Sam said quietly.

"How does she know?"

This was the hard part. "She says she got Pa to tell her one time."

"That's the only thing I believe so far," he said. "Pa would tell anybody but us."

There was silence as the waiter set their plates down on the table. Michael speared a sausage with his fork. The juice ran out on his plate.

"I didn't believe her at first but now that I've thought about it for a while, I've decided she's right," Sam said. "Remember all those times she hid in her room when we came home from school? And the times we came here for dinner with Pa? The way she used to talk to him. And think about her face. It looks—" He stopped, searching for the right word. "—Degenerate. As if something's eating away at her."

Michael didn't say anything. Sam could see he was piecing things together slowly.

"I bet she was drinking when she had the accident," Sam said slowly. "She kept stopping that day to go into bathrooms and coffee shops. I bet she had the bottle in her purse."

"Wait a minute," Michael said. "You're getting a little dramatic. Have you seen anything around the house? Any bottles stuck in the wastebasket?"

Sam shook his head. "She must keep them in her room. She wouldn't leave them around for us to find." Suddenly Sam felt he had to convince Michael. It all seemed to fit so perfectly into place.

But Michael was not yet convinced. "I won't believe it

until I see it," he said angrily.

The noise in the restaurant increased suddenly as a group of teenagers wrestled their way through the crowded tables. The manager shouted something at them in Italian, and the kids burst out laughing.

Michael smiled. "This is what you and I should be like," he said waving his hand behind him. "Loud and honest. Everything up front. You would go home now, knock down Ma's door, and confront her. 'Hey, Ma,' you'd say, 'if you're going to drink, why don't you do it out here in the open?'" Even Sam had to smile at that picture of himself.

"That's why I like working down at the church. When Father Fitzgerald's angry with someone, he just hauls off and yells at them. Everybody knows where they stand. None of this sneaking around, muttering things about each other." Sam didn't answer.

"Let's go," Michael said suddenly. "I don't think we should leave Ma for too long."

They paid the bill and walked out. The narrow cobbled streets of the North End were teeming with people. Children dodged up and down the street, chasing each other through groups of old men gathered around the domino boards and women hunched together on the stoops.

Sam and Michael didn't speak to each other on the bus or during the long walk up the hill. As they rounded the corner at the bottom of Winthrop Street, Sam glanced at the house. The light in Ma's room was still on. From the monument they heard shouts of laughter and then the splinter of breaking glass.

Sam walked up the steps to the house quickly. He turned to look at Michael.

"Aren't you coming?" Sam asked.

Michael shrugged. "I thought I might go down to the

church and see what's going on," he answered quietly.

They were both silent for a minute. Sam never could get away from the house, and Michael dreaded going into it.

"You're scared of what we're going to find," Sam said. "For all your talk, you're just as scared as me."

Michael did not answer him. They stood there in the ringing summer night, waiting. After what seemed like years, Sam opened the door, and they saw what they had been afraid to see.

Ma was crumpled up on the bottom step, her eyes closed, her body leaning against the wall.

"Michael," Sam cried out, scared that he had already left. But Michael was standing right beside him.

"What are we going to do?" Michael whispered, and for once Sam felt like the older brother he was.

Sam touched his mother's shoulder and pushed her gently. Her head rolled over to the other side. He leaned over and called to her. "Ma, wake up, Ma." He could smell the liquor. He felt as if he were looking at a dead person. Her hair looked dried out and tangled and her face was gray. Sam shuddered. How many times did Pa have to look at this behind those closed doors?

"Sam, we've got to do something," Michael said.

"Come on the other side of her, and we'll take her back upstairs."

"Is she—" Michael stopped.

"No. She's just passed out. I can feel her breathing."

Between them, they were able to get her up the stairs although it took a long time.

"I can smell it," Michael said as they tried to straighten the bed around her. "She smells like the bar down on Main Street."

The thought made Sam smile.

"They aren't any different, you know," Michael said in response to the smile. "A drunk's a drunk."

"Come on, Michael. Ma is not the same as those men who sit in the bar all day."

"You're right. She's worse. She hides away in her bedroom all day. A typical Everett wife. Keep the skeletons in the closet."

Sam didn't want to argue with him so he said nothing.

"I'm kidding, Sam," Michael said gently. Sam nodded and looked away. It always surprised him when Michael softened.

There was a silence. They didn't know whether to go or stay.

"I guess she's all right for now. There's nothing else we can do," Sam said tentatively.

Michael pushed open the closet door and began rummaging around on the floor.

"What are you doing?" Sam asked.

"Looking for the bottles. If she wants to start again, she'll have to come out to get her liquor."

They found the bottles. They were stashed in funny places all over the room, some never touched and some empty. After a while, Michael went out to the kitchen and got a cardboard box which they filled to the top.

"I feel like a burglar," Sam whispered as he opened the top bureau drawer and picked carefully through the underwear. Every once in a while one of them would check their mother as she moved in her sleep, but she never woke up.

Between them they carried the box downstairs and around to the back where the garbage cans were lined up.

"She's got mostly bourbon and vodka," Michael said as he took the bottles out and lined them up.

"She can always go out and buy more," Sam said sadly. He shivered though the night was warm. The sky was black and absolutely clear. Two years ago we would have been in Maine right now, he thought. He jumped at the sound of breaking glass. Michael was hurling the bottles at the brick wall just above the open garbage can. He handed Sam a bottle.

"Your turn, old boy," he said with a gleam in his eye. "Have a shot. Don't step over the line. Wolfschmidt Vodka. Only the best."

Sam took aim and hurled the bottle at the wall. It broke and fell with a crash. They took turns stepping to the line, taking aim, and throwing each bottle carefully so the splinters fell noisily but neatly into the can. Sam rejoiced in the noise and destruction of this odd ritual. "That felt great," he murmured to Michael as they shook hands solemnly after the last loud crash.

"That's more noise than Charlestown has heard since last night," Michael said with a grin as they let themselves in the front door.

Sam went up to his room and climbed onto the window ledge. The street down below was dark except for the muted glow of the streetlights. There was the occasional sound of a voice on the square and the soft hum of distant traffic.

"I feel betrayed," he said aloud, aware of how dramatic it sounded. He stopped his thoughts for a moment and rearranged them so that he thought about one person and one thing at a time. First, there was Ma. His feelings about her were so scattered and abrupt that it was hard for him to arrange them. He hated her for what she was doing to them. He felt like her father suddenly instead of her son. He wanted to tell her to pull herself together, to start acting like a mother.

He thought of Pa, and that same old loneliness came

over him again. It was worse this time because he and Pa had not been to each other what he had always thought they were. The biggest secret of all Pa had not told him. Did he think I was too young, that I couldn't handle it? Sam wondered. Or worse than that, was Pa just too scared to admit he couldn't handle it, too scared to ask for help?

Sam heard Michael come up the stairs and go into his room. Sam thought of going in to him but he didn't know what to say. There was a fragile truce between them now, but it had always been broken before.

He got into bed and lay there listening to the summer night sounds. It was a long time before he fell asleep.

9

The next morning Sam went down to her room and tested the door. It was locked from the inside. He knocked softly but there was no answer. For a terrifying moment he thought something had happened to her, but then he heard the soft scrape of a drawer closing.

She came out around lunchtime, dressed in a pair of pants and a shirt. Her hair was combed and she had obviously tried to put on some makeup although the line of her lipstick was blurred. Something was different. She had stopped drinking. She didn't say anything to him but Sam just knew.

They spoke to each other as if nothing had happened. That was the way she obviously wanted it and Sam was too relieved to see her sober to say anything.

"But don't you think we should say something?" Michael asked.

"Maybe later. I don't want her to start again." He shrugged. "Maybe it won't happen again."

"I bet that's what Pa always said to himself," Michael answered. " 'I won't tell the kids this time. Maybe it's the last time.' "

"Are you going to say something to her?" Sam asked.

"No. I'm scared to," Michael said simply.

So that was the way they left it.

The time went by slowly after that. It was as if they all lived in the ocean. The crest of each wave came when Ma was sober, and they believed she wouldn't drink again. And then the crest would roll by, and they'd slip down the long side of the wave to the bottom as she disappeared back into her room.

Sam had avoided Kathleen for a couple of days. He didn't know what to say to her. He was still angry, but he knew it was Pa who had disappointed him, not Kathleen. As it turned out, they ran into each other on the street.

She looked as if she were going to move on down the sidewalk but he stopped her.

"Can I talk to you?" he asked.

"I was just going to the church," she said, avoiding his eyes.

"I'll walk with you," he said, falling into step beside her.

Neither of them talked for a while. For once Kathleen had been grateful for Peggy's snooping, because she'd learned what had been happening over at Sam's house in the last couple of days. She already knew about the smashing of the bottles. And Peggy told her that Mrs. Everett had gone out to shop for groceries one morning, so Kathleen knew she'd sobered up at least for a while.

"How's your mother?"

Sam shrugged. "Sober. For the moment." There was a pause. "I'm sorry. I didn't mean the things I said. I was just so angry with—" He hesitated. "With everybody, I guess." He wanted her to stop walking and look at him. He wanted to try and see what she was thinking.

"It's all right," she said softly. "It was a hard thing to have to hear. For a lot of reasons."

They were already at the church. "Could we sit on the steps for a minute?" Sam asked. "You don't have to go in right away, do you?"

"No. I can talk to you for a minute."

They were silent, looking out over the old training field in front of the church. Two mothers were sitting on the benches watching their children climb over the big cannons.

"What happened? Did she just stop drinking?" Kathleen asked.

"That night, Michael and I went out to dinner and I told him what you'd said. He didn't believe it either at first, but when we got home we found her passed out at the bottom of the stairs. She must have fallen down them. We put her to bed, and then we looked through her room for the bottles. We filled a whole cardboard box with bottles. Mostly bourbon and vodka."

"What *was* all the noise that night? You must have woken up the whole neighborhood."

Sam grinned. "Target practice with the bottles. It made us feel great to hear all that glass breaking. It won't make any difference though. She can always go out and buy more."

"Maybe this is the last time," Kathleen said, although she didn't believe it, and she was sure Sam didn't either.

He didn't answer. There was something else he wanted to ask her.

"When Pa told you about her drinking, he didn't tell you how it started, did he?" It hurt Sam to admit to that special relationship between them again but he was curious. "Maybe if we know what sets her off, we can help her."

"No. He just told me she was an alcoholic. I think he might have known about my father, although he didn't mention it."

"I wish my grandmother were still alive. She'd know what to do."

"What about that aunt of yours? The one who was at the funeral?"

"She's not the easiest person to talk to," Sam said slowly.

Kathleen stood up just as the door behind them opened. Michael looked out. "I thought I heard voices. What is this? A secret meeting place?"

Kathleen felt herself blushing. It was as if she and Sam had been caught at something.

"Is Father Fitzgerald here?" she asked.

Michael nodded. "He's in the office. Want to come in, Sam?"

"No, thanks. I've got to go back," he said, waving up the hill vaguely. "See you later."

"Sam acts as if he might catch some disease in here," Michael said.

"I guess he doesn't want to compete with you," Kathleen said as she headed down the hall to the priest's office.

"I guess you're right," Michael said to himself.

The days grew hot and breathless. Sam felt suffocated in Charlestown. Kathleen was taking extra courses at the college through the summer so he didn't see much of her. On the days Ma was sober Sam couldn't bear to be in the house with her, pretending that everything was just fine, and that they were hiding nothing from each other. On those days he went out wandering. He would get on the bus in the morning and stay there until he saw something interesting. He saw parts of Boston that he never knew existed, and he would come home at night exhausted. His mother seemed disturbed by him.

"Where do you go all day?" she'd ask sharply. "You

need a job. You need something to do, some interest like Michael. What about your photography? We bought you that fancy camera, and I never see you use it anymore."

So he began taking the camera with him just to get her off his back. Some days he walked down by the Charles and watched the people along the river. He never spoke to the kids his age. It was always the old people or the little children. He didn't know himself why he was doing it. Maybe he was just lonely for someone to talk to.

On the days she was drinking, Sam stayed home.

"I don't get you at all," Michael said. "Those are the times you should clear out. She's okay to be with when she's sober."

Sam shrugged. "Someone should be here, in case she needs help."

"She'll never ask for it," Michael said. "She'll die in that bedroom before she comes to either of us."

Michael was right. She didn't ask for help. They rarely spoke to one another on those strange separated days they spent together in the house. But Sam stayed and listened and waited much the way he had when his father was sick.

She had never gotten around to fixing up Pa's study for herself, and the room had a bare echoing sound that Sam didn't like. One day he opened the cupboard door and found Pa's things piled up on the shelves. He began to take them out one by one and put them back on Pa's desk, until it looked the same old way again. Sam sat there in the late afternoons and stared out the corner window down Winthrop Street to the old training field. Pa must have sat here those July afternoons when they were in Maine, and he came home to an empty house.

"Did you hate her, Pa?" Sam asked the desk. "Did you ever think of leaving her? I wish I could leave now. But there's nowhere to go. A person can't divorce his mother." His words echoed against the bare bookshelves. "You should have told me, Pa. You shouldn't have left me like this without any warning at all." Suddenly, he began to shake. He picked up a photograph of his parents on their wedding day and stared at it. Their younger happy faces looked back at him and told him nothing.

A shiver ran up his spine and, without turning around, he knew she was standing behind him. Slowly he put the picture back down on the desk.

"Bunch of crap," she said blurrily.

"What, Ma?" he asked loudly, turning around to glance at her. She was glaring at the picture.

"'In sickness and in health till death do us part,'" she recited in a high-pitched, whiny voice. "Bunch of crap. I kept all the promises. He didn't."

"Don't drag him down with you, Ma," Sam said suddenly. "Leave me somebody to respect, will you?"

"Your father wasn't the saint you thought he was, Sam," she said slowly.

"Maybe not. But I don't want him dragged through the mud now that he's gone." Sam's hands were shaking. He put them down on the desk.

"What about me, Sam? Nobody ever cares what happens to me."

"Yes we do—"

"Oh, shut up," she interrupted. "I'm tired of hearing about it."

"Shut up yourself, Ma," he cried at the slammed door. He ran upstairs and slammed his own door, just to fill the silent house with noise.

10

Michael stopped by to see Kathleen one day after rehearsal. She came to the door and agreed to walk around the monument with him.

"I'm worried about Sam," he said. "I thought maybe you could talk to him."

"What's wrong?" she asked.

"Well, he's acting really strange. The days that Ma is sober he disappears. I don't know where he goes, but he comes in after dinner looking kind of glazed and exhausted. He takes his camera, but I know he doesn't take any pictures. Then on the days that she's drunk and locked in her bedroom, he stays in the house and waits for her to come out." Michael shrugged. "I guess that's what he's doing. I've tried to get him to come down to the church, but he won't get near the place. We really could use some help with the props, but he thinks I'm just creating a job for him."

"How is your mother?" Kathleen asked.

"Pretty bad," he said. "She used to go on binges—I guess that's what they were—when she'd lock herself in her bedroom for a couple of days or longer, and then she'd be sober for a few months or more. Well, now she's sober one day and drunk the next. I think she's getting better at disguising the drinking, too. For all we know, she may be drinking every day."

They walked for a while in silence.

"I know we should say something to her," Michael said slowly. "But frankly, I can't face it. I don't think anything we say will really make any difference. And the thought of having to tell my own mother that we know she's a drunk gives me the creeps. So we both just avoid it."

Kathleen smiled. "You don't have to explain it to me. It all sounds very familiar. I tried to talk to my father once, and it was a disaster. It seems to me that an alcoholic really knows better than anyone how to get under your skin. They have to get to you before you can get to them. That's what Father Fitzgerald says."

"Does he know a lot about alcoholism?" Michael asked.

Kathleen smiled again. "Go ask him. You'd be surprised how much he knows."

"All I want to do is get away from it. Every man for himself. If Ma wants to drink herself to death, that's okay. I just don't want to go down with her."

In the silence that followed, Michael could feel Kathleen looking at him curiously.

"I guess I don't feel that strongly," he admitted. "I do care what happens to her but I feel kind of helpless right now, so I just get away from it. And that's what I think Sam should do."

"All right, I'll try to talk to him," Kathleen said. She had been avoiding Sam, she admitted to herself.

She stopped by at the house on the way home from school the next afternoon. Sam looked pleased to see her. They walked upstairs quietly past his mother's open door. She was lying on the bed fully clothed.

They sat down on opposite ends of the window ledge.

"How is she today?" Kathleen asked quietly, pointing downstairs.

"Sober, I think," Sam said. "But frankly, it's getting harder to tell the drunk days from the sober ones. I think she's drinking every day now. It's a strange thing to watch. A sort of slow disintegration." His face looked thin and tired.

"Why stay here to watch?" Kathleen asked. She could see now why Michael was worried about him. "It must be creepy to be here with all the memories of your father and then watching her wandering around."

"Sometimes I wish I had X-ray vision and could see right through that bedroom door when she closes it," he said.

"Why? What do you want to see?"

"What she's doing. I want to see if she drinks it straight from the bottle or whether she bothers with a glass. Is she sitting on the bed or wandering around? Does she have any clothes on? Does she read anything or do anything all day long?" Sam knew how strange and morbid his words sounded, but it was the truth.

"I never had that problem," Kathleen said, looking across the street at her house. "My father's always come parading in, swinging the bottle and singing." She tucked her legs up, conscious of his eyes on her. "There are books about alcoholism, you know. Why don't you read about it? A lot of doctors think it's a chemical disease. There's something in their chemical makeup that makes them drink. They can't help it."

"I don't believe it," Sam said. "Do you?"

"I'm not sure," Kathleen said. "It does give them an excuse, I guess."

Downstairs they heard footsteps walking along the hall. Sam walked quietly across the room and closed his door. When he came back, he sat down next to Kathleen.

"I'm worried about you," she said slowly. "I wish you'd get out of here more. Why don't you go back to your photography?"

"Not you, too," he groaned. "Have you been talking to Michael?" He didn't wait for an answer. "I don't feel like taking pictures right now. I don't feel like doing anything. But it's nice to have you worry about me," he added softly as he reached out and took her hand.

He had never touched her before. She didn't say anything, and she didn't move her hand.

"I've missed you," he said quietly, watching her face.

Before she could answer, they both heard the footsteps again, this time on the stairs. Kathleen jumped up and started walking out of the room. "I've got to go," she said as she opened the door. Mrs. Everett was standing on the landing looking up toward her.

"Sam, I want to talk to you alone, please," she said in a cold voice. "Good afternoon, Kathleen," she added in a tone that meant good-bye rather than hello.

Kathleen nodded and ran down the stairs away from all the tension in the dark house.

Sam sat on the window seat and waited for his mother. She came in the room and glanced around. They both realized that she hadn't been upstairs in a long time.

"What do you want?" Sam asked, aware of the rudeness in his voice.

"I don't think Kathleen's mother would like you two up here alone."

"Why not?" Sam asked. He knew exactly what she meant but he wanted to hear her say it.

"Because it's not right. At your age, you should not be entertaining girls in your bedroom," she said stiffly.

Sam laughed, a low, hollow sound. "Doesn't it feel a bit odd, Ma, for you to stand there and tell me what's right and what's not right? It seems to me you've given us the right to do anything we damn well please. Judging from how you've been acting and all."

"What are you talking about?" she asked angrily. She looked at him sharply as if trying to judge something from the expression on his face.

She really thinks I don't know, Sam thought to himself. How incredible.

"Nothing," he answered. "Just don't tell me what to do anymore, all right? I can take care of myself, thank you. You take care of yourself, and I'll take care of myself." He turned away and stared out the window.

"Don't you ever talk to me like that again, Sam Everett," she shouted. "Just because your father is dead doesn't mean you can treat me like a piece of trash. I'm your mother and I lay down the rules around here until you grow up. And for your information, sixteen years old is not grown up yet. Now you can just stay in your room and think about that for a while."

Sam didn't turn around. She went out closing the door behind her.

After that, Sam made one more try before giving himself up to hating her. He went to see Aunt Holly.

"Why bother?" Michael asked when Sam told him of his plan.

"I think it's time we knew a little more family history," Sam answered with a wry smile. "I'd like to know when the drinking started, and if Pa ever thought of getting a divorce. You know, all the gory details," he added with a gleam in his eye.

"You find it all sort of fascinating, don't you?" Michael asked.

Sam didn't answer for a minute. "I'll tell you what it's like," he finally said. "Like a photograph coming up slowly when you put it in the developer. First you see just a blurred image, and then slowly the lines become more distinct and the shadows lighten up, and all of a sudden the whole picture is right there in front of you. All these years we've just been seeing a blurred picture of Ma. Now that I know the truth I'd like to know the whole truth."

"You can try," Michael answered. "But I doubt Aunt Holly will tell you anything. She probably doesn't even admit Ma has a problem. If she admitted that, she would have to do something about it."

But Sam went anyway. When he walked into the tall dark front hall, it reminded him of all the times they came here to see Grandma.

Sam had put on a good pair of pants but he could feel Aunt Holly looking at him disapprovingly.

"Uncle Theodore isn't home yet," she said busily as they walked into the upstairs sitting room. "I hope he'll get a chance to see you." Sam nodded. He and Uncle Theodore never had much to say to each other. "We both feel badly that we have not seen more of you this summer," Aunt Holly went on. "Things have been so busy here and then, of course, we've been away. We're going out to the Cape next week with the Russells."

Sam began to wish he had never come. Aunt Holly seemed determined to rattle on to him as if he were one of her Beacon Hill friends who had come for lunch. How was he ever going to ask her what he'd come to ask?

Jane brought in the tea tray and put it down noisily. Sam smiled at the pained look on his aunt's face. She hated noise and things out of place and untidy people.

She used to dress her two daughters like dolls. They talked that way too, in stiff polite voices. "They sound as if they've been wound up," Michael had once said. "Turn the key, give them a push, and they walk and talk just like real little girls."

"How is your mother?" Aunt Holly asked suddenly, stirring her tea vigorously with a spoon. "I've tried to reach her on the phone, but there's never any answer."

"She's not doing very well," Sam said slowly as he put his glass down on the table.

"Yes, it must be hard for her," Aunt Holly said quickly. "Especially since you all are stuck way out there in Charlestown."

"I think Ma doesn't care where she is right now." Sam stopped and waited for his aunt to ask him what he meant. She looked down at her lap and smoothed out her skirt. She's not going to make this any easier, Sam thought.

"She's drinking a lot," he said very quietly, watching the reflection of his face in the mirror across the room. His lips had barely moved at all.

"Yes—well, we had expected that," Aunt Holly said. "The pressure on her must be tremendous." She reached up and slipped a piece of her brown-gray hair behind a bobby pin. "And she must be awfully lonely," she said softly, looking off at something behind Sam's head. "I know she has both of you, but it's different without Charles." She stopped and closed her eyes. She loved Pa too, Sam thought as he looked at her. With all we've been through, I did forget that.

"But Aunt Holly," he prodded gently, "it's worse than that. Michael and I know now that she's an alcoholic. You don't have to hide it from us anymore."

Aunt Holly's face tightened and he could see the muscles around her mouth move.

"I think that word is awfully strong, Sam. It's true she used to have a little problem, but things have been much better. She was so good all through your father's illness, so strong."

"She's started again," Sam said sharply.

"I'm sure it's not as bad as—" She stopped.

"As bad as what?" Sam asked, leaning forward. He felt as if they were tiptoeing along a tightrope together. If only he could get her to tell him. "Tell me what it used to be like. Tell me when it started."

Jane came in suddenly, and Aunt Holly leaned back against the pillows of the sofa. Jane scemed to take forever to put the tray together and take it away. When the door finally closed behind her, Aunt Holly's face still had that vague, distant look. Neither of them said anything for a long time.

"She was different when he first brought her here," Aunt Holly said quietly. The late afternoon sun was slowly crawling across the flowers of the old rug. Sam settled back into the deep cushions of his chair and relaxed for the first time that afternoon. She was going to tell him the story. "She was such a quiet girl, nervous and shy. We all tried to be friendly, to bring her out, but our family is so loud and restless and—well, we just drowned her out, I guess. You knew your grandmother," she said, focusing in on him for a minute. "You had to shout at her the things you wanted her to know. She wasn't deaf. She just had so many people and books and pictures to think about." Aunt Holly sounded sad as if she had missed something too. "We were surprised when he said they were going to get married. The other girls had been cheerful and talkative, and Deborah seemed lost and sad. Not his type at all." Sam smiled, remembering that Pa had once told him he liked Ma because she knew how to be quiet. "She didn't talk at you, she sat back and listened. It was a charming quality to find after all those yackers."

"So you see she never really fit into his crowd," Aunt Holly was saying. "She couldn't keep up with them, so she started to drink to relax. And the more she drank, the worse it got."

"What do you mean?" Sam asked quickly.

Aunt Holly waved her hand impatiently. "Well, she got loud and couldn't concentrate on what people said, and she laughed at all the wrong times. Everybody began to notice, and I guess your father spoke to her, but she wouldn't stop. So Mother did something about it."

Downstairs the front door slammed. Aunt Holly sat up very straight again. "Your Uncle Theodore is home," she said a little nervously. They waited in silence as he came up the stairs and opened the door.

"Well, you two certainly look guilty," he said loudly as he clapped Sam on the back. "How are you, Sam? I'm glad you came over for a visit. We haven't seen enough of you since—" He broke off and walked across the room. Uncle Theodore was always saying the wrong thing. It seemed to go with his bluff way of talking and his square, tweedy figure, but it jarred with Aunt Holly's neat, precise speech and manners.

"What have you two been discussing?"

Aunt Holly looked down at her lap and straightened her dress for the third time. Even her nervous habits were precise.

"Aunt Holly was telling me about Ma. What she was like when Pa met her." Sam stopped. "And about her drinking."

Uncle Theodore looked surprised.

"Sam should know," Aunt Holly said quickly. "Deborah has started drinking again, and Charles is not here to shield the boys anymore."

Theodore shrugged as if to say, it's your business. There was an awkward silence.

"What did Grandmother do?" Sam asked.

"It was at the big Christmas lunch. Your mother was worse than ever. I think she must have been drinking before they came, and your father had this terrible, tight expression on his face. There were about twenty of us around the table, and we all tried to keep up the conversation and cover things up for her, but her voice was always the loudest and she kept saying mean things about Lydia, who was sitting right across the table from her."

"That was awful," Uncle Theodore murmured from his stand by the fireplace.

"She kept reaching across the table for the wine decanter. We all knew we should stop her, but we didn't know how. We didn't want to make a scene. Finally Mother couldn't stand it anymore, and when Deborah reached for the wine again, she stopped her. She just said very loudly, 'Deborah, you have had enough wine.' I remember we all stopped talking and looked down at our plates. Mother never minded making a scene. Deborah's face looked very white, and she sat back in her chair and didn't say a word for the rest of the meal. And that was the last time I saw her drink. You see, after that, she always did it in secret. You could tell she'd been drinking, but she never touched alcohol in front of us. It was almost worse because she made us all pretend that she was all right. Rather than confront her and make a scene, we helped keep her secret. Especially after Mother died." Aunt Holly shuddered.

In the silence that followed, the mantelpiece clock chimed six times. From downstairs there came the distant sound of curtains being drawn and rattling silver.

Uncle Theodore turned around suddenly. "Gosh, it's

getting late," he said. "I must change."

Sam stood up to go. He wanted to say one more thing. Aunt Holly was stacking the teacups noisily.

"Could you talk to her?" he asked them, not daring to look directly into either of their faces.

"It wouldn't do any good," she said quickly as if she had anticipated the question. "You see, we've tried to before. It makes her angry. It almost makes things worse," she ended lamely.

"There's no one else," Sam said. "I don't think she has any other family."

Aunt Holly was looking at him carefully. He knew she was wondering whether he could talk to Ma.

"I can't do it," he said simply, and she nodded. Neither of them wanted to try and convince the other. They said good-bye and he walked slowly to the bus stop.

"It was sad," Michael said when he heard the story. "Ma must have felt so lost and alone. She told me that her parents had just died, and she came North to get away from the memories."

But Sam didn't feel sorry for her anymore. He knew he should care, but when he thought of her, he saw only her nervous tired eyes and heard only her sharp, biting voice.

"I guess I'll go to bed," Sam said without moving. Michael wondered if Kathleen had said anything to him.

"I'm going to talk to Father Fitzgerald tomorrow about Ma. Kathleen says he knows a lot about alcoholism."

"What good's that going to do?" Sam asked, getting up slowly. "Ma thinks he's trying to convert you down there anyway."

"We should talk to someone who knows something about the problem," Michael said. "It can't hurt."

"It won't embarrass you to have him know she's a drunk?" Sam asked slowly.

Michael shook his head. The idea hadn't even occurred to him.

"I was just wondering. Someday I'll have to come meet this priest of yours," Sam said as he started up the stairs. "Good night."

11

Father Fitzgerald did not seem surprised when Michael asked to speak to him privately.

"Sit down, Michael," he said, waving at a backless chair on the other side of his desk. The desk was piled high with papers that slid easily onto the floor or into the various cardboard boxes that had never been unpacked. There was a small hot plate in the corner of the room, where a kettle simmered for coffee or tea. Among the sea of papers, there were usually two or three cold cups of coffee that Father Fitzgerald had forgotten about.

"What can I do for you?" he asked. "Do you want a cup of coffee?"

"No, thanks," Michael said. "I want to talk to you about my mother. I came to you because Kathleen suggested it."

"What's wrong with your mother?"

"Well, since Pa died, we've discovered that she's an alcoholic." Michael looked down at his hands. They were shaking, which surprised him because he actually felt relieved to have told someone.

"Are you sure, Michael? That's a pretty strong word to

use. Does she just take an occasional drink, or does she go on binges?"

"Right now she seems to be drinking all the time," Michael said.

"Why don't you try and describe her behavior to me?"

So Michael described the events of the last few weeks, everything he could remember from the smallest detail to the way she looked the night they found her at the bottom of the steps. The priest listened without saying anything, his feet propped up on the desk, his chin resting on his folded hands. When Michael was finished, he leancd back against the wall, and there was a moment of silence between them.

"Whew, it sounds like you and your brother have had a bad time of it."

"It's worse for Sam than it is for me," Michael said. "I can come down here, but he doesn't have a place to go." Michael shrugged. "He always lets himself get more wrapped up in the family problems than I do. But that's not the point. What do you think about Ma?"

"Well, it sounds to me like she's a classic alcoholic. That poor woman," he added softly. "She must be going through hell." Michael was surprised by the pain and pity in his voice. He didn't say anything.

"I could sit here and lecture you for a couple of hours on alcoholism, but frankly I think the whole thing will be much clearer if you come to a meeting in the church hall this evening. We meet at eight right after the rehearsal is over, so you could just stay."

"What kind of meeting?" Michael asked.

"I'm not going to tell you," the priest said with a grin. "If you're mystified, you'll be sure to come."

"All right," Michael answered. He got up reluctantly. He had been hoping for some solution, for more of an answer.

"There aren't any easy answers to this problem," Father Fitzgerald said gently. "Alcoholism is a disease, but the trouble is that most of the time the patient doesn't want to be cured." He stood up. "It's even worse than that. Most of the time the patient won't even admit he's sick."

Michael didn't pay much attention to the rehearsal that night. He kept watching Father Fitzgerald, looking for some sign from him, some further explanation, but the priest spent his time trying to walk Kevin through his part. At quarter of eight, he dismissed the cast and motioned to Michael to follow him. They went through a side door into a smaller room where some folding chairs were set up. On a side table, a coffee machine had been plugged in and two or three people were gathered around it. They greeted the priest warmly, and he introduced Michael. Michael recognized some of the people as they filed in the back door. There was Mrs. Sullivan, Kathleen's aunt, and Mr. O'Neill, the Saturday postman, and Connie MacLeod, one of the big politicos in town. There were others too that he didn't know. He glanced at Father Fitzgerald curiously, but the priest said nothing. After everybody had taken a chair, Father Fitzgerald raised his hand for silence.

"I have a young friend here who I thought would be interested in our meeting tonight. I haven't told him yet why we are here because I thought together we could do that better. John, I believe I asked you to lead the meeting this week." A large man sitting near the front of the room stood up and turned his chair around to face the group. He glanced over at Michael.

"Good evening. My name is John, and I am an alcoholic." He waved his hand at the group. "That's why we're here. We're all alcoholics. Or married to them. Or friends of them."

Michael studied the faces turned toward him. Some of them were smiling at his surprised expression.

"But you're not drinking now," he blurted out, thinking of Ma locked up in her room.

John shook his head. "No, but we could start again at any moment. That's why we're here. To stop each other from taking that first drink. Because for all of us, there's never just one drink. That's what makes us alcoholics. I'll tell you what happened to me. I grew up in New York. My father was a carpenter, and my mother died when I was very young, so us kids had to take care of each other. I started drinking beer in high school just like the other kids. But I was different. I never could stop after one beer. I had so many that my friends were always carrying me home. I joined the army and things stayed under control for a while, but on weekend leaves we drank the hard stuff. Sunday mornings, I'd wake up in strange places and I could never remember what had happened the night before. After the war was over, I got a job as a janitor in a high school. The trouble was I never could start the day without that little bottle of whiskey I kept hidden in the basement locker, and by the time the kids arrived I was usually passed out in my office. When they fired me from that job, I swore I would stop. I met a girl, and we got married and everything went along fine for a while. I actually stopped drinking for a whole year. Then we went out one night to celebrate our anniversary, and I thought, well, I'll just have one beer. One beer won't hurt. But as soon as I got that taste in my mouth, I wanted another and another. My wife had to call my best friend to take me home. It went on like that. I would stop for a while but there was

always a reason to start again—someone had been rude
to me, it was cold that day, I had nothing to do for an
hour." John smiled. "An alcoholic can find any good
reason to drink." Some of the other people in the room
murmured assent. "Well, we moved up here thinking a
change of scene would do me good. But the whole thing
started all over again. Finally, my wife left me and, a year
later, I ended up in a hospital. I don't even remember
how I got there. That's where Father Fitzgerald found
me. He brought me to these meetings, and I haven't had
a drink for two years—and twenty-seven days, to be
exact." He laughed at the look on Michael's face. "When
you're an alcoholic, the first thing you think of every
single morning is that drink. So I count all the days that I
go without it."

"I remember when I was counting the hours," a
woman said loudly.

"So do I," said another woman.

"Do you want to tell us about it, Ann?" John asked.

Ann shook her head.

"All right then, some other time."

"Michael, do you have any questions?" Father Fitzgerald asked.

Michael shook his head. He had lots of questions, but
he didn't know which ones to ask first. Deep down, he
was disappointed. The man's story had been interesting,
but what did that have to do with Ma? he asked himself.

"We meet every Tuesday and Thursday night," John
explained. "You are always welcome to join us for the
first part of our meeting. The second half is open only to
alcoholics."

From the looks on the people's faces around him,
Michael understood that he was supposed to leave now.

"Thank you," he managed to say as he stood up and
left the room.

When Michael came to Father Fitzgerald with some of his questions, the priest put him off gently. "Come to some more of the meetings," he suggested. "After a while you'll begin to see a pattern. The pattern will seem familiar."

So two nights a week Michael stayed down at the church after rehearsal for the first hour of the meetings. The more he heard, the better he understood. Each person told a different story, but certain details were always the same.

"I kept thinking I would just have one little drink, but one drink was never enough. So I would have another and another until I passed out."

"I thought I was so funny. At parties, I was always laughing and telling jokes. I saw my wife watching me with this sad look on her face, but could I help it if she didn't have any sense of humor?"

"Nobody ever dared talk to me about my drinking. They all just kept hoping I would get a hold of myself. To them, an alcoholic was just a disgusting, morally weak person with no willpower. That's what I thought too, until I came here and found so many other people. That's when I began to realize that I had a disease."

After these meetings, Michael would wander home in a daze, hearing and rehearing all those stories. He watched Ma more closely, and he began to suspect she was drinking more than they realized. Her replies to questions were often vague and nonsensical, and she'd begun to make mistakes all the time. She knocked a hot frying pan off the stove, she left out the sugar when she baked some cookies, she forgot to meet a friend for lunch. She was in and out of her room all day long, and Michael was sure she was secretly drinking every time she went in. She came out smelling of perfume and mouthwash.

"Bourbon smells better than that stuff," Sam said.

"She is just barely functioning," said Michael. "She doesn't do anything around the house anymore, and she hasn't had anyone for dinner since the month after Pa died."

"Who would want to come?" Sam asked with a thin smile.

One night when Michael sat down in the back of the room he was surprised to see Father Fitzgerald stand up and turn his chair around. He glanced over at Michael and smiled in a sad way.

"I think it's time some of our newer members heard my story," he said in a loud, clear voice. "I am no better and no worse than anyone here because I too am an alcoholic."

Michael was so stunned that he did not hear the priest talking for a while after that. He had always assumed that Father Fitzgerald sat in on the meetings because he had formed the group. It had never occurred to him that the priest might have been through what everybody else was describing. He sat up and listened.

"By that time, I was so low, so desperate for a drink that I begged money. And the minute someone gave me a dime or a quarter I was off to the Lucky Lady, where Frank the bartender gave me credit. As long as I came in with something, he would pour me a drink. There I was, the great boxer of Charlestown, down in a bar in the South End, shaking so badly that I couldn't even lift my fist, much less a boxing glove. My own mother wouldn't have known me. Thank God," he added with a smile. There were answering smiles from around the room. "But Father Donohue knew where I was, and he kept coming back to look for me. He wouldn't leave me alone no matter what hole I tried to hide in. And one night when he couldn't find me anywhere, Frank sent him to the city hospital where I had been taken in after a fight in the bar. I woke up in a straitjacket. I couldn't move my fists. I was helpless."

"Alcohol is a straitjacket," said a voice in the front row. Michael couldn't see who was talking.

"That's right," said the priest. "That's what I finally learned after four days in the hospital. I went home with Father Donohue instead of back to the Lucky Lady."

There was applause from the other members of the group and Father Fitzgerald suggested they break for coffee. He started back toward Michael's chair, but Michael left the room before the priest could reach him.

When he walked out the door of the church hall, he turned right, away from home, and walked down one of the steep streets to the main part of town. He didn't want to go home for a while. He needed some time alone to think.

He stayed out very late that night, wandering up and down without looking where he was going. Finally he ended up sitting on the monument steps watching the lights of Boston across the harbor.

Oddly enough, his thoughts kept returning to Pa. He hadn't thought about his father much since he died. He'd tried to put him out of his mind because everything about their relationship seemed unclear to him, unfinished. They'd disagreed about small things because they were scared to argue openly about bigger questions. Besides, Sam was always at Pa's side, and Michael was reluctant to tag along. So more often than not, Michael had gone off alone.

Once he met the priest, Michael had not felt so alone, so left out. He sensed a kinship there that he had never felt with his father. Somehow the news that Father Fitzgerald was an alcoholic hurt him more deeply than his own mother's problem.

He avoided the church for the next few days even though it meant missing some important rehearsals. But finally he decided it was silly to run away, and he went down to talk to the priest.

"I'm glad to see you, Michael," Father Fitzgerald said quietly when he saw him standing outside the office. "We've missed you at the rehearsals."

"I'd like to talk to you."

"All right." The priest stood up and stretched. "Can we talk and walk at the same time? I'm tired of being cooped up in here."

They took a couple of turns around the training field without speaking. The priest had a long stride for a short man, and Michael found himself working hard to keep up.

"Now I feel like some lunch," Father Fitzgerald said, clapping Michael on the shoulder. "Let's go down to Annie's diner. The omelettes aren't bad."

"I didn't bring any money," Michael said.

"My treat. She lets me charge," Father Fitzgerald explained with a smile.

Halfway down the street, he brought up the subject they had both been thinking about.

"I expect you were surprised by my story at the meeting the other night."

Michael nodded without looking up.

"You didn't know I was an alcoholic?"

"No. I just thought you had formed the group so you were allowed to stay."

"But that would be breaking the first rule. Nobody can stay for the second part of the meeting unless they are an alcoholic." He paused. "Does it amaze you?"

"Yes, I guess it did at first. But I've gotten used to the idea."

"But you were disappointed, weren't you?" the priest asked without looking at him.

"Yes," Michael said.

"I'm flattered that you care that much." There was no sarcasm in his voice, and Michael didn't know how to answer. They didn't say any more about it. Over lunch, the priest asked Michael if he thought Sam would come to the meetings.

"I've told him about them but he doesn't see what good it's going to do Ma," Michael answered.

"I think it will help you to understand a little bit about the nature of the disease. If you boys understand some of what she's going through, it might help you talk to her. Does she have any other family?"

"Not really," Michael said. "Sam won't admit it's a disease. He thinks that makes things too easy for her. He really hates her."

"Try to bring him down, Michael. The more you both understand, the easier it will be for you to deal with her. And the easier it will be for you to separate her alcoholic self from her real self."

Michael sighed. "We haven't seen her real self in so long, I've almost forgotten how nice she can be."

"That's just what I mean."

A couple of days later to Michael's surprise Sam finally agreed to go to a meeting with him. "I'll do anything to stop you from bugging me about it," he muttered as they walked down the hill.

When Father Fitzgerald saw them come in, he nodded at Michael without coming over. Then he stopped and spoke to the young woman named Ann. When the meeting started, she was the one he had chosen to lead it.

"I started drinking at home because it was the right

thing to do. My parents always had wine at dinner, and from the age of sixteen, I was given a glass to learn how to drink properly. Little did they know that after they'd gone to bed I'd sneak downstairs and pour myself some more. Alcohol made me feel great. I loved everybody, I was pretty, I was interesting. I started to drink even more when I went away to college and for a while everything was fine. I was dating a lot of boys, and they all loved the way I could 'hold my liquor' as well as any of them. But all the time, I was craving alcohol more and more, and it got so I couldn't get through the day without a drink. My roommate moved out after a while, telling me I had a real problem. I told myself she was just a prude and I was lucky to be rid of her. But then even the boys stopped asking me out, and I ended up sitting alone in the town bar. Sometimes I went down there before my classes, and those days I never got to class at all. I called home and told my parents that I wasn't feeling well, and I didn't like college. So they let me come home, and I sat in my room and drank the liquor that I stole from my father's bar. My parents must have known what was going on, but they closed their eyes to it." She laughed bitterly. "I needed help but nobody was willing to admit it, least of all myself. Then one day, I was arrested for speeding, and the police gave me a test for drunken driving. My father smoothed everything over, and they sent me to a psychiatrist who prescribed a lot of pills. Soon I was hooked just as badly on pills as liquor. It wasn't bad all the time. Some months I'd stop completely for a while. But the craving was always there and once I broke down and took that first drink, there was nothing stopping me until I passed out. Well, in one of my good times, I met a man and fell in love." She looked down at her lap. "He didn't drink, so I stopped too. Everything was beautiful for a while without the liquor, but then

one night I started again and he saw me at my worst."
She was quiet for a minute. "He brought me here. It
turned out that he was an alcoholic too. He knew how
low you could sink because he had been down there."
She stopped and Michael thought she'd finished, but she
lifted her head again. "I've learned from coming here
how much we all need each other. When you're in that
crazy world, living from one drink to the next, the only
person you can listen to is another alcoholic. Someone
who has been down in that hell too." She stopped again.
"That's all," she added with a little smile. The group
burst out clapping.

"Why are they clapping?" Sam asked Michael.

He smiled. "Father Fitzgerald has been trying to get
her to tell her story for a long time. She has always held
back. It must be a hard thing to get up in front of all
these people and tell a story like that."

They listened to two other people speak and then,
during the coffee break, Michael told Sam they had to
leave. "The rest of the meeting is for alcoholics only."

Sam glanced around the room as they went out the
door. "Your priest is staying," he said. "Don't tell me he's
an alcoholic, too?"

Michael didn't answer for a minute. It was a hard
thing to admit even though he knew now it was a disease.

"Yes, he is. He hasn't had a drink in a long time, but
he calls himself an alcoholic because he still has the
craving."

They walked up the hill in silence. Michael felt a
strange sense of relief. As they opened the front door,
Sam stopped. "That woman, Ann—"

Michael nodded.

"—she said the only person one alcoholic will listen to
is another alcoholic," Sam finished. "Do you think that's
true?"

Michael smiled. "Well, if it is, it certainly lets us off the hook, doesn't it?"

They heard footsteps moving along the hall above them. Her bedroom door closed, and they could hear the bolt sliding across.

"I still hate her," Sam said quietly. "I don't think anything will change that."

"I feel sorry for her," Michael answered as they walked up the stairs to the kitchen. "From everything I've heard in the last few weeks, I realize she'll never be able to stop by herself."

"Would Father Fitzgerald talk to her?" Sam asked.

Michael poured himself a glass of milk. "I've thought of that," he said slowly. "I know he'd do it if I asked him to. But you know how horrible Ma can be. She hates the Catholics, she looks down on the Irish, she doesn't like Charlestown. . . ." His voice drifted off.

Sam's face softened. "I understand," he said simply.

12

It was not long after that that things seemed to change for the better. One morning, Ma came out for breakfast for the first time in weeks. She sat with them at the table and watched Sam cooking the eggs without saying anything.

Her hair was limp and hung straight down around her face. Although she had obviously put on makeup, the powder did not cover the deep wells under her eyes or the way her face had bloated up around the cheekbones. Her clothes were tight in some places and loose in others, and she didn't seem to notice the spots on the front of her blouse or the way her wraparound skirt pulled apart when she sat down. She smelled like sweet perfume. Michael shuddered. He wondered if she'd ever been this bad when Pa was alive. He wondered whether Pa would even recognize the woman sitting at the table with them.

Sam poured her a cup of hot coffee and set a plate of eggs in front of her. She picked up a fork and pushed them around the plate.

"They look good, Sam," she said apologetically. "I'm just not hungry."

He nodded.

"I didn't realize you could cook," she said.

"I learned this summer," said Sam pointedly.

"I have left you two to fend for yourselves quite a bit, I suppose. But you're both pretty grown-up," she added breezily. "I knew you could cope with things."

Sam opened his mouth to say something else but Michael cut him off. "How are you feeling now, Ma?" he asked.

"Oh, I'm much better. I thought I'd go over to Cambridge and do some shopping today. Meet a friend for lunch or something."

"That sounds great." Michael disliked the false tone in his own voice but he persisted. "Is there anything we can do for you?" He flinched at her look. "I mean, shopping or helping you with the mail?"

"I am perfectly capable of running this house without your help," she snapped. "Just because I've been—" She faltered. "—I've been preoccupied doesn't mean you two can just take over."

"Sorry, Ma," Michael said angrily. "I didn't realize you were so jumpy." He stood up and his chair scraped loudly. "Well, Sam, I guess your days in the kitchen are over," he remarked loudly as he went out the door.

Sam put some dishes in the sink and stood there for a long time watching the water run over them. He didn't want to look at Ma. For once, he found himself wishing she'd go back to her room.

"He has a mean streak in him," Ma said coldly. "Just like your father."

Sam started at her words. He felt as if he'd been slapped in the face.

"Pa did not have a mean streak in him," Sam said.

"Your beloved father was not all he was cracked up to be," she muttered. "For your information, the good Doctor Everett could be a perfect shit when he wanted to be."

"Hey, Ma—" he started in a casual voice. "Don't you ever shut up?" he shouted as he ran down the stairs away from her.

That was the day he first went to the church. As he left the house, he knew he wanted to talk to someone, and without really thinking about it, he went looking for Michael.

"If I hadn't left then, I think I would have hit her," he told Michael when he found him backstage.

"I don't think she even knows what she's saying," Michael said.

"I don't care if she drowns in that bottle now."

"Good morning, Sam," said Father Fitzgerald as he came up behind them.

"Hello," said Sam without turning around.

"Ma was sober this morning," Michael explained in a quiet voice. Kevin and Patrick were standing out on the stage practicing their lines.

"Sober, but not very pleasant," Sam added.

"Alcoholics can often be harder to deal with when they're sober. They act like cornered dogs, striking out at everybody else just to protect themselves."

"Hey, let's start," Patrick called.

"Come be the audience with me," the priest said to Sam. "We need a fresh eye on this play."

Sam sat and watched them rehearse the play twice. He was thinking of getting up to leave when he heard Patrick yell at Michael, "That brother of yours. Does he say anything?"

Michael grinned. "He walks. He talks. I guarantee

you. You just have to press the right button."

"Oh, shut up, Michael," Sam called from his chair.

"See what I mean?" Michael said. "I know all the right buttons."

Sam felt like marching out of the room but he knew how stupid that would look. Besides, he was enjoying himself. There was a comfortable feeling in the room because they were all working on something together. He hadn't realized how much he'd been by himself this summer.

"Do the last scene again," Father Fitzgerald called to the actors.

"You're kidding," Kevin said. "That's the third time this morning. I've had it."

"Well, if you concentrate instead of horsing around, you might get it right this time. Sam and I are getting a little bored ourselves." He turned to Sam. "What do you think of it?"

Sam was silent for a minute. "Patrick and Michael are very good. And that girl who plays Pegeen. But what are you going to do for sets?" Sam knew the first performance was only a couple of weeks off.

"That's a problem. We need something in the background, but we don't have enough money to buy anything." He shook his head. "I haven't concentrated on that problem very hard."

"If you want," Sam said slowly, "I could try and throw something together."

"Really?" the priest said with a smile. "That would be great." He jumped up and stopped the rehearsal. "Players," he announced in a dramatic voice. "Meet our new set designer."

"Now, wait a minute—" Sam said. He was embarrassed to have them all staring at him.

"He talks," Kevin said in mock surprise. "Did you see that, my friends?"

"Shut up, Kevin," Patrick answered. "I think we need him after all." They gathered around arguing with Sam about what the set should look like until Sam gave up even trying to say he wouldn't do it. Secretly, he was pleased and nervous.

"But I've never done anything like that," he said to Michael on the way home.

"You helped Ma with the backdrop for the stage up at the Point."

"But this is different. They want a complete Irish inn right down to the last bottle. And it's supposed to be ready in just a few weeks."

Michael clapped his brother on the shoulder. "Sam, my boy, if anyone can do it, you can."

"You sound like Pa," Sam muttered.

"I was trying to," Michael answered with a grin. "And listen, if you need any extra bottles, I know just where to find them."

But Sam didn't even hear the joke. He was already drawing things up in his head.

He spent one whole day sitting in the back row of the auditorium planning the set. Once his design had been approved by the rest of the group, he asked Michael where to look for wood. "Father Fitzgerald says we don't have any money to spend on it," he complained. "How am I supposed to get the materials?"

"Tell Patrick what you need," Michael said. "He'll know what to do. Just don't ask him where he gets the stuff."

Sam talked to Patrick and the next morning there was a huge pile of lumber in the back of the auditorium.

"There's enough here to build three sets," Sam said to Michael. "And some of it's brand-new."

"Will that be enough?" Patrick asked, coming up behind them with a wide smile on his face.

"Where did you get it?" Sam asked.

Patrick looked up at the ceiling with folded hands.

"The Good Lord doth provide," was his only answer as he walked away.

"And the Good Lord may taketh it all away again," Michael said as he turned over a two by four. "Look at this."

The lumber was stamped RIDGEWAY HARDWARE.

"You mean he stole it?" Sam asked.

"What did you think he was going to do, buy it?" Michael asked. "Now let's move it backstage before someone comes looking for it."

Father Fitzgerald had scheduled lots of rehearsals, so they were both spending most of their days at the church. Ma seemed curious and a little jealous, although they were all relieved not to see too much of each other. "Especially since none of us are talking about the thing we are all thinking about," Sam said to Michael.

"What do you do down there all day?" Ma asked one evening when they came in late for dinner.

"Sam's constructing the set, and the rest of us are rehearsing," Michael said as he sat down at the table.

"And what does the priest do?" Ma asked with a note of contempt in her voice.

"He supervises," said Sam shortly. He thought of saying more but a look from Michael stopped him. It would do no good to start an argument with her about Father Fitzgerald.

"I'm sure your school friends are home. You boys

ought to call them up."

"We're too busy now, Ma," Michael said.

"I'm going to be pretty busy myself," Ma said. "I've signed up for some classes at B.U. with my friend Mary Chadwick." She smiled at them coyly, like a little girl with a good report card. Sam looked away.

"That's great, Ma," Michael said quickly. "Which classes?"

"Two on art history. I thought maybe I might get a job in that area someday." She fingered her napkin nervously.

"Why don't you start painting again?" Sam asked.

"Well, it's time for me to be practical, now that your father's gone. I'll never be able to make any money with the painting. I'm not good enough at it."

She wants us to say she is good enough, Sam thought. I'm not going to give her that satisfaction.

"You could be good if you did it every day," Michael said.

She stood up to clear the table without answering.

"Who is Mary Chadwick?" Michael asked as they went up to bed.

"She's the one who moved up from the South about ten years ago. Ma went to school with her down in Savannah. Remember she came to lunch at Grandmother's one Sunday, and Aunt Lydia imitated her accent behind her back, and I heard Grandma tell Pa that she had such a plain face?"

Michael shook his head. "We come from a family of snobs," he said angrily.

"Well, we never pretended to be anything else," Sam said with a smile.

Kathleen first heard from her brothers that Sam was doing the set.

"Are you sure you don't mean Michael?" she asked.

Andrew shook his head. "No. It's Sam. Father Fitzgerald convinced him to do it, and Patrick pinched some wood for him."

"Amazing," Kathleen said as she went into the kitchen. She poured herself a glass of milk and hurried upstairs when she heard her mother's key in the back door.

She hadn't seen Sam since the time Mrs. Everett had found them upstairs. It was funny the way their summer had gone. The days had passed without their seeing each other and yet, she had to admit, she thought about him a lot.

"I really do like him," she said out loud, listening to her own words and wondering about them. She had never had a boyfriend like other girls in Charlestown. In high school, she'd concentrated on studying so she could get into college with a scholarship. She'd spent her free time with Dr. Everett and Sam, or down at the church with Father Fitzgerald. The boys she'd gone to school with thought she was a snob, and so she avoided them.

Kathleen stood at the window and looked down the street. Her courses at the college were finished until the fall. Maybe she would go down and see if she could help out with the play.

Michael saw her come through the door, and he jumped down from the stage to meet her.

"Have you come to help?" he asked eagerly.

She nodded. "I heard from Andrew that Sam's down here. I couldn't quite believe it." She glanced around the room looking for him.

"It's true. Father Fitzgerald got him to agree to do the sets." Michael jerked his thumb toward the back of the stage. "He's down here all day, hammering and sawing.

He's a changed person. Did you ever say anything to him?"

"I tried to. We were interrupted by your mother." Kathleen blushed and looked away. She wondered what Michael thought of her and Sam.

"Kathleen!" Sam had spotted her from up on the stage. "Come see what we're doing," he called. She smiled at the way he looked. His sleeves were rolled up, and his dark hair had fallen over his forehead.

"I've come to help," she said as he led her backstage. "I'm through at the college until the fall."

"Terrific," he said with a smile. "There's lots of work to do. We are expected to construct a full-scale Irish tavern in the next ten days. Now, here's my office," he explained as they came to a pile of lumber. "And here's the way I've drawn it up. We'll use the two-by-fours for supports and save the plywood panels for the front of the bar. What are you laughing at?" he asked.

"Nothing really," she said. "You just look great. It's nice to see you wrapped up in something other than your mother's problems."

"Isn't it appropriate that I'm constructing a bar?"

"Appropriate for both of us, considering our family tendencies."

"I'm glad you came down," he said softly. There was a silence between them. Father Fitzgerald broke it.

"I see you're pulling workers in off the streets now, Sam," he said as he came up behind them. "I know she can wield a pen, but the question is, does she know how to use a hammer?"

"She'll get plenty of chances to learn," Sam said. "Now leave us to our work, please."

In the days that followed, Kathleen and Sam spent all their waking hours together, side by side on the floor, sawing, hammering, arguing over the design. Sam was surprised at how well Kathleen could visualize the set. Often she could see much better than he how to give the audience a feeling of something without actually building it. Gradually, to everybody's amazement, the stage was being transformed into the Irish public house in the play.

One morning Kathleen wasn't at the church as usual. Sam found it hard to work without her. He sat and watched Michael, who was looking through the costume collection backstage.

"We wore the same stuff last time," Michael said in an irritated voice. "It's amazing how this one pair of pants can do for a king and an Irish peasant."

Sam smiled. "This company operates on a shoestring, my boy. You've got a set this year. Last time, as I recall, the backdrop consisted of a black curtain with a couple of lines on it for windows."

"It is incredible what you've done," Michael said, glancing at his brother.

"I couldn't have done it without Kathleen. She is really good at something like this. Wait till you see what she figured out for a fireplace."

"You two do an awful lot of talking over there. Are you sure it's all about the set?" Michael asked with a grin.

Sam didn't answer. More than anything else, he knew he was enjoying the chance to be with Kathleen every day, working on something together. Sometimes when she was bent over a board concentrating on her work, he'd stop what he was doing just to watch her.

The side door opened, and Sam went out to see who it was. Kathleen was struggling, pulling a wooden crate into the room. He jumped down from the stage to help her.

"Where've you been?" he asked.

"That's heavy," she said, leaning the crate against the wall. "I dragged it all the way down Winthrop Street. You should have seen the looks I got. Your mother thought I was completely crazy."

"My mother?" Sam said. "She's supposed to be at class."

"She was just going in the house with another lady when I went by. She didn't introduce me," Kathleen said with a hint of sarcasm in her voice. "Well, what do you think?" she asked, pointing at the crate.

Sam looked at it blankly. His mind was still on his mother.

"It's great," he said. "What is it?"

"Sam, you are hopeless. It's our fireplace. Help me carry it backstage and I'll show you."

"Where did you get it?" he asked.

"I found it in the Ryans' backyard. But don't tell anyone." She grinned. He noticed again the way her eyes changed when she smiled.

"Do we have another felon on our hands?" he asked. "What with you and Patrick, I've got the basis for an unflattering character profile of the Irish people."

They set the crate down carefully. "I rang the bell but nobody was home, so I just took it."

"And where did you get that, Kathleen Murphy?" thundered a voice from the wings. Kathleen jumped behind Sam.

"O glory be," she cried in an Irish brogue. "Your big brother is sure to murder me now, Samuel."

Michael burst out laughing. "Don't let Father Fitzgerald hear you, my girl, or he'll put you on the stage."

She sat down on the edge of the crate.

"Kathleen said she saw Ma going into the house with another woman," Sam said.

"But I thought she was going to class this morning,"

said Michael, looking puzzled.

"So did I."

"Oh darn," Michael said, dropping down beside Kathleen. "We can't be her baby-sitters."

"Maybe the class was canceled," said Sam, but he knew how feeble it sounded. "I wish she would just get herself under control. I'm sick of thinking about her."

Kathleen glanced at Michael. That's a healthy sign, she thought. Three weeks ago Sam would have still been sitting up in his room, listening to his mother tiptoe clumsily around beneath him.

"I told you I don't think she can do it by herself," Michael said. "She needs help. Maybe we should speak to Father Fitzgerald," he added softly.

"Not until the play is done," Sam said.

Kathleen raised her hand. "Wait a minute, you two. She may still be off the bottle. Why don't you find that out before you jump into something?"

Sam and Michael looked at each other. Neither one of them wanted to go home and face the false, bitter person they were sure would be waiting for them.

"Don't do it now," Kathleen said. "Michael's right. You can't be her baby-sitter. Finish here today, and worry about it when you get home. My new rule is, don't let your local alcoholic ruin your life." Her voice sounded bitter. Sam had heard from Andrew that their father was drinking heavily again.

There was a silence. The side door opened and slammed shut again. Patrick jumped up on the stage. He looked surprised to find them sitting on the crate in the dark.

"Well now," he said, "isn't this sweet? What do we have here? A convention?"

Nobody said anything.

"What's this old piece of trash?" he asked, giving the crate a kick. "Kathleen's been scrounging again."

"You must have a bad one on this morning," Kathleen said sharply. "No sleep at all, I would guess, after the noise I heard up at the monument last night."

"Your father was the loudest of us all," Patrick spat back.

"Oh, so you're drinking with the big boys now," Kathleen muttered. Her eyes narrowed. "You don't have to tell me about my father. I heard the shouting when he finally came home. But you're starting even earlier in life than he did. I hope no silly girl falls in love with your handsome face before she sees that bottle you've always got clutched to your bosom." And with that, she walked off into Father Fitzgerald's office and slammed the door. The three boys watched her go in silence. Sam was amazed. He had never heard her speak that way before.

"She inherited that sharp tongue from her old hag of a mother," Patrick growled.

"I guess her mother's got good reason," Michael said coolly. "Come on, Sam, I'll help you drag this to the back." They left Patrick standing by himself, staring up at the stage.

13

They both kept putting off going home that night. It was getting dark when they unlocked the front door. The house was quiet.

"Ma," Sam called softly from the top of the stairs. There was no answer.

"She's not here," Michael said when he turned the kitchen light on. "She left us a note. 'I've gone to a movie with Mary Chadwick. Will be back late. Dinner in the icebox,'" he read.

"I guess that's good," Sam said, opening the refrigerator door. "It's meat loaf." He pulled out the pan and cut off a piece. After the first bite, he made a terrible face and ran to spit it out in the garbage.

"What's wrong?" Michael asked. "You look as if you've been poisoned."

"She put hot pepper in it," he gasped between gulps of water. "Or something like that. Don't try it. You'll die."

Michael sniffed at it tentatively and threw the whole thing into the garbage. "Peanut butter and jelly again," he said slowly.

"She wouldn't have done that on purpose," Sam said.

"You mean she wouldn't have done that if she had been sober," Michael answered.

Sam shrugged. They ate in silence, listening to the sounds of the house.

"Let's make a list," Michael said suddenly.

"What?"

"A list of all the times she's done something like this. You know if we ever confront her with the drinking, she's going to deny it. That's what every alcoholic tries to do. Cover it up. So we've got to have the evidence. A complete record."

Sam opened his mouth to say something but Michael cut him off. "I don't know if we're ever going to face up to it. But at least this way, we'll be ready."

Michael tore a piece of paper off the telephone pad and got a pencil from the drawer.

"Now, let's start from as far back as we can remember. Even before Pa died. All those strange hamburger dinners with her hiding out in the bedroom. And we'll be very specific. Dates and descriptions if possible."

Sam laughed. "You sound like a general planning his battle campaign."

"That's what I feel like." Michael shrugged. "It sounds kind of crazy, but at least we're doing *something*."

They sat there for what seemed like hours, remembering times together.

"There was that time she had all her hair cut off, and Pa didn't even notice."

"I don't think he liked it," Sam said. "I thought it looked horrible too."

"That was the trouble. She thought she looked much prettier, and he just deflated her by not even saying anything. Now when was that? I remember I had Mr. Morse in school because he had just called them in for an appointment about me, and she wore a scarf which looked really stupid. So that must have been in the sixth grade."

"Do you remember the time she poured herself some wine at dinner, and he knocked the glass out of her hand?" Michael nodded. "And the time we were upstairs listening to a dinner party, and she came stumbling up and found us?"

"When you complained about having to go to bed, she slapped you," Michael said slowly.

Sam nodded. He remembered how shocked he'd been, more by the twisted angry look on her face than by the way his cheek stung. She was really hitting someone else, he thought now. Pa maybe, or herself.

"What about when Pa was sick? She was sober all that time, wasn't she?" Michael asked. "I wasn't around much then."

"I'll say," Sam said wryly. He thought for a minute. "I think there was one time," he said. "She caught the flu that first winter and she complained about how bad she felt. When I mentioned it to Pa, he just shrugged and said, 'Well, at least she knows she's not going to die from it.' At the time, I remember thinking how cruel it sounded. And she just disappeared for a couple of days. Pa looked grim and wouldn't talk to me or anything. He knew what she must have been doing. But she was all right when she came back."

"Pa must have been a hard man to be married to. Grandma brought him up to be so self-centered," Michael said.

For once, Sam didn't argue.

They went to bed quite late but Ma still hadn't come home. In the morning her door was locked, and she didn't come out of her room for breakfast.

"Guess it's another bedroom binge," Sam said as they walked down Winthrop Street that morning, and Michael agreed.

But to their surprise she was up and sober at dinner-time, although the old nervous twitch in her neck was back.

"Did you find my note?" she asked. "I see the meat loaf is gone. You boys must have been hungry."

"We had to throw it out," Michael said.

"There was some kind of hot pepper in it," Sam explained. "You must have taken the wrong spice off the shelf."

"How strange," Ma said, looking confused. "I don't remember—" She didn't finish the sentence.

"What movie did you see?" Sam asked. Every question seemed loaded just because of the things they weren't saying.

"It wasn't very good," she said shortly. "We had dinner afterwards so I was late coming back." There was a silence.

"I saw your friend Kathleen yesterday morning," Ma said. She always called Kathleen *your* friend. "She was dragging some huge old box down the street. She looked absolutely crazy."

"That's part of the set for the play," Sam said. "She's helping me."

"The first performance is Saturday night, Ma," Michael said.

"Oh yes, I've written it down. I'll be there."

But she wasn't. "I was relieved," Sam admitted to Kathleen. "She's so unpredictable. But I think Michael was hurt. I saw him watching the audience come in from the stage door."

Michael had been angry with her and then angry with himself for caring. For the first time, he missed Pa. Pa had always been there in the front row, carefully watching his son's every move. When Michael was younger, it had made him nervous, but later on he began to appreciate the careful criticism Pa offered. "An actor in my family," Pa had once said proudly. "I never would have believed it."

The first performance went well despite the fact that Patrick had had a few drinks to steel himself and had forgotten some of his lines.

"I've seen him act this part stone cold sober," Sam whispered to Kathleen at the back of the auditorium, "and he really is not as good."

She frowned. "Don't ever tell him that. Patrick doesn't need any more excuses to drink."

"Why does his drinking bother you so much?"

"Because I'm sure that's what my father must have been like once," she said softly. He reached over and took her hand.

The set did look authentic and Sam was pleased with it. Before the play started, they had decided to hang a curtain over the doorway leading to Pegeen's bedroom. In the second act, Patrick tripped over the curtain and Sam held his breath as the doorframe swayed back and forth. But it held.

Michael was very good. Sam was surprised at how completely he changed into the character, especially since the part was a hard one to act.

"Michael should get a better part next time," Sam said to Kathleen when they were applauding at the end. "He's just as good as Patrick."

Kathleen nodded. "I know. But as long as Patrick wants to do it, Father Fitzgerald will give him the lead. He's Irish, the plays are always Irish, and Michael's not Irish."

Sam knew she was right but he hated to admit it. He had begun to feel at home down here. For the first time, Charlestown no longer seemed like just some part of Pa's history books or the place he went to after school.

Looking at the actors taking their bows, he realized that now the play was over, he had no excuse to come down here. The thing they had all worked on so hard was almost done. He glanced at Kathleen, who was watching the stage intently. She would be going back to college, and he started school again next week. He knew he'd miss the easy, close times they had shared in the last few weeks.

Without this place to come to, he'd be creeping back up those stairs past the closed bedroom door again. He felt as if finally he had broken out of the dark shell of that house. Soon it would close back down around him.

"I hate this feeling of something ending," he said to Michael on the way home that night. "It's the same way I used to feel when we left the Point after Labor Day."

But Michael wasn't really listening. He was still reliving the play.

"Did you notice the part where Molly slapped Patrick? That wasn't in the play at all." Michael grinned. "I think she was just trying to bring him back to his senses. He was quite drunk this time. But all the same, he was still good."

"I think you're just as good," Sam said.

"Do you really?" Michael asked. Then he looked away, embarrassed.

"I do. I wish you could get the lead sometime."

"Not as long as Patrick's around." Michael shrugged. "Maybe I'll get some good parts at school this year. The sophomores are always more involved."

They were walking slowly, retracing the path they had walked so often in the last few weeks. It was dark, and the streets were empty for a Charlestown summer night. The houses that sloped up Winthrop Street seemed to lean against each other for support, all of them tilting up toward the monument. It was still warm but there was a breeze, just enough to stir the fat, green leaves in the park, just a hint of fall. When Sam turned to go into the house, Michael stopped him.

"Let's go up to the monument and look at the view," he said. "I don't want to go in yet."

Sam nodded. They climbed the steps and stood at the base of the stone spire. Down below, across the harbor, the lights of Boston spread out along the two rivers. The city seemed far away and quiet. Michael sat down on the top step. His brother's voice broke the silence. "I remember when Pa first brought me up here to look at this view. He told me we were going to move into that house on Winthrop Street and I remember thinking, but why should we move at all?" Sam smiled. "I never said anything, of course. When Pa was enthusiastic about something, it seemed cruel to break into his mood."

"I missed Pa tonight," said Michael. His voice sounded bitter. "It would have been nice to have had *someone* there."

"It's probably better that she didn't come, Michael. If she'd been drunk, she might have made some awful scene." Sam sat down beside him.

"She gets away with murder. We spend all our time worrying about what's happening to her, and she goes merrily along without a thought for us," Michael said. "Sometimes I wish she would just go away and leave us alone."

Sam knew how he was feeling. The two of them seemed to go up and down on this seesaw over Ma. Just when one brother was feeling a little sorry for her, the other began to hate her all over again. And she probably has no idea what effect she has on us, he thought.

"Do you remember how she was in the summers up at the point?" Sam said softly.

"She was at peace with herself then," Michael replied.

He picked up a stone and scratched faint white lines in the cement.

"Do you think she'll ever be that way again?" Sam asked.

"I don't know," said Michael. He stood up and threw the stone. It hit the street below with a faint click. "Right now I think she might kill herself first. One way or another."

They started for home. "What we've got to figure out is how to keep her from ruining our lives at the same time," Michael said.

Sam nodded in the darkness. At least we're going through it together, he thought to himself. Finally.

14

It felt strange to be back in school. Sam went from one class to another as if he'd never seen the place before. His mind was somewhere else and he couldn't believe the summer was over. He was not even surprised when the headmaster called him in, because it was all just part of the dream.

"Sit down, Sam," Mr. Adams said, nodding at the one empty chair. "I hope you had a good summer. You were up in Maine?"

"No, sir. We had to sell that house when my father got sick." Sam knew he could have let the man off easier. But he got a certain pleasure out of embarrassing him. Mr. Adams was usually in control of the situation.

"Oh yes, of course. I had forgotten that." He pulled his chair forward and flipped through some papers.

"Sam, I'm afraid we have not received any payment from your mother for either last term or the present one. Ordinarily, I wouldn't talk to a student about a problem like this, but I understand that in your case there are special circumstances."

That means he knows she drinks, Sam thought. The old Beacon Hill gossip mill.

"I spoke to your mother on the phone about this two or three times last summer and she was very understanding and said she'd mail the check soon. But we haven't received anything yet." Sam nodded, remembering the bare desk in Pa's old office and the piles of papers that sat untidily on Ma's bureau.

"Now if there is any problem about the money"—Mr. Adams stopped and cleared his throat, but Sam was silent—"then of course, we would be happy to talk to your mother about some kind of loan or scholarship. You and Michael are both doing well here, and we would not want to lose you."

There was a silence, and Sam realized he was supposed to say something. "I'll talk to her, Mr. Adams," he said slowly.

The headmaster stood up. "Your mother must have a lot on her mind these days."

"She should," Sam muttered as he went out. "But she doesn't."

The first thing Michael did when he heard about the meeting was to pull out their list. Their special list had become a kind of obsession with him, and Sam had to admit that he also got a certain satisfaction from reading it over. "It's all there," he said to Michael. "At least we have a record."

Ma's drinking methods had changed again. She had not gone on one of her ten-day binges since the middle of the summer. If she was not up when they left for school, she managed to pull herself together enough to have dinner with them every night. But the boys knew she hadn't stopped. The signs were there in the gray smoothness of her skin and the careful way she walked and the strange jerks of her head. Their conversations together were careful and halting, and the two brothers felt a sense of relief when they could finally escape upstairs to their rooms.

"It's almost more painful this way," Sam said. "At least when she disappeared, we didn't have to keep up these false conversations every day."

"Why are we such cowards?" Michael asked once again. "Why don't we just sit down and talk to her about it?"

"Because any time we've come close to talking about it, she's exploded." Sam shrugged. "I'm scared of her. When she's like this, I almost believe she could pick up a gun and shoot us. She's not in control anymore. The liquor is." They were silent for a minute. Michael seemed to be thinking over what Sam had said. "I'll never forget that man in Father Fitzgerald's group. The one who ran over his own grandson and killed him. He was going out to buy more bourbon."

"We're going to have to do something about the school bill," Michael said.

"I thought we might go through that pile on her desk and just pay it."

"But she has to sign the check," Michael pointed out.

So Sam brought the subject up at dinner the next night.

"Oh, yes," she said vaguely. "I believe somebody called about that. I'm sure I paid it."

"I'll get the mail from your bureau," Michael said, jumping up. "We can pull it out." He left the room before she could say anything.

The pile of mail told more than anything else how she had lost control of things. There were bills from the month after Pa died, unopened letters, notices from the bank. Most of the stubs in her checkbook read cash, and the running balance had not been kept up. To Sam's surprise, she did not object to the two of them sorting through the pile.

"I have let things go a little," she mumbled as she

cleared the table around them. The boys said nothing. Sam was opening the bills, and Michael was sorting them out.

"The bank must put money into the account every month," Sam said. "See these yellow deposit slips? Is that right, Ma?"

She nodded. "Your father set up the system when he got sick."

"Open the statements," Michael said. "So we can balance the checkbook."

Sam glanced up at Ma. She was wiping the top of the stove, the sponge going around and around in the same big slow circle. Some time later she left the room but the boys did not even look up. Michael was struggling with the checkbook.

"Boy, is this a mess," he said. "The trouble is she didn't keep a complete record of the checks she wrote, so that even though it looks as if she had a lot of money in July, she was actually overdrawn that month. And she did pay some bills back in June. In fact, she paid the phone bill twice. Here's the credit slip."

"There's nothing here from the liquor store," Sam said quietly. "Pa used to have a charge there."

"I bet those are all the checks written out to cash." Michael flipped through the bank notices. "There are two months here when the bank transferred more money than usual. Pa must have set that up so that we'd have enough to pay the big bills like tuition and the taxes. But she spent most of it. There's only enough in the account now to pay half the school bill, and that would wipe her out until the end of the month."

"We can't handle this ourselves," Sam said. "I'm going to call Uncle Theodore."

Sam took the mail with him to school the next day, and on the way home he stopped at his uncle's house.

Uncle Theodore had come home early to meet him. They sat down at the big front desk together, and Sam showed him everything. He made some notes on a pad and told Sam to leave the papers there.

"She obviously can't handle this all herself," Uncle Theodore said as he showed Sam to the door. "I know your father was hoping to avoid paying an accountant, but I don't think there's any other way now. Don't worry. I'll call her tomorrow about this."

Ma didn't ask them where the papers had gone. She seemed quite cheery at dinner and told them a story about one of the students in her art history class. "And then the little bitch uncrossed her legs and sat there all slouched down in the first row. Well, the teacher paid no attention at all. Mary and I roared with laughter." Ma began to laugh loudly again, ignoring the stares of the two boys.

"That sounds pathetic," Michael said as he picked up his plate.

Ma stopped laughing so abruptly that Sam was reminded of a windup bear he had been given for Christmas one year. One flick of the switch and the animal stopped banging, his drum handle poised in midair.

"You two are so serious these days," Ma grumbled. "You make me nervous."

They left quickly.

Sam was the first one home from school the next day. He got a glass of milk out of the icebox and was walking up the stairs when Ma opened the bedroom door.

"Just a minute, Mr. Smart-ass. What do you mean by showing all my private mail to that uncle of yours? Now he wants me to meet with some damn accountant who's going to tell me how to run my life." Sam watched as she grabbed hold of the banister rail. Behind her, he could see the vodka bottle standing on the bureau.

"You haven't paid any of the bills, Ma—"

"Don't you tell me what to do," she shrieked, starting up the steps after him. Her face was contorted, her mouth an angry hole. "I can do whatever I damn well please." Sam turned and ran up the stairs. He slammed the bedroom door behind him and leaned against it, humming loudly to himself to drown out the shouts from the bottom of the stairs.

When Michael came home, he found Sam locked in his room.

"Her door is closed now," Michael said after he heard Sam's story. "Come on."

"Where are we going?"

"To see Father Fitzgerald. Someone's got to talk to her."

The priest was in his office. He smiled and waved when he saw them coming through the auditorium door.

"Where have you two been? I've missed you." He took a closer look at their solemn faces. "What's happened?" he asked quickly. "Is it your mother?"

"We were wondering if you'd talk to her," Michael said. "She's really gone out of control. She hasn't paid any of the bills since Pa died, and she's drinking every day now. She looks horrible. Her face is all gray, and her clothes are always dirty."

"And she uses this awful language." Sam shuddered. "She's beginning to act like some wild animal."

The priest leaned back and ran both hands through his hair. "I thought you might say something to me this summer. Why did you wait so long?"

Michael sank down in his chair. "We didn't want to spoil everything. And the play distracted us. We didn't have to see so much of her then."

The priest frowned at him. "Spoil what?"

"She can be so ugly," Michael said. "If you go there—" He paused. "We don't know what she'll say to you."

Sam sat watching the two of them look at each other. Michael has found someone to replace Pa, he realized suddenly. He pushed away the feeling of jealousy that rose up in him.

Father Fitzgerald was smiling. "So you wanted to protect me?" He shook his head. "There is nothing that your mother can say that I haven't heard before. Or said to someone else myself. For heaven's sake, don't worry about that."

He was silent for a minute. "Do you think she's drunk now?"

Sam nodded. "Definitely."

"So when's the best time to catch her sober? If things are this bad, I don't think I'll get through to her when she's drunk."

"About ten or eleven in the morning," Michael said. "She usually doesn't get up before we go to school."

"So she's probably feeling pretty bad in the morning. Hung over and hating herself all over again."

"Tomorrow morning, she's supposed to see an accountant with my uncle," Sam said. "So maybe you should wait another day."

"I'm beginning to think it's hopeless," Michael said. "But if it goes on much longer, I'm moving out. I can't stand it. How do you live with someone like that?"

"Ask Kathleen. She knows better than anybody." Father Fitzgerald leaned back in his chair. "You live your own life as much as you can. Stay away from her. Don't feel guilty about anything that happens to her. Nobody can stop her from drinking but herself. An alcoholic is the most deceitful person on earth. He deceives himself, and he does his best to deceive other

134

people. So as long as you go on pretending with them, you're just making things worse."

"What do you mean?" Michael asked.

"Here's an example. Your mother never came to the play, did she?"

"No."

"But you had told her about it. So what was her excuse for not making it?"

"She said something about being sick," Sam said. "We just ignored it."

Michael remembered her face that day. He had wanted to slap it. "I'm so sorry, Michael. I felt sick, so I stayed in bed." There had been a short silence, and Michael had turned away to go downstairs. "I have this terrible cold coming on," she had added nervously. "But there's another performance tonight. Maybe I'll feel better by then." He had turned back and stared right at her, and he remembered now the way she'd shrunk from him. It seemed as if some curtain had been lifted from her face. She looked scared and helpless. And then that sly look dropped down over her again.

"Don't bother, Ma," he shouted much too loudly as he ran down the steps. "I don't really want you to come anyway."

"Now that's the time when you should be honest with her," Father Fitzgerald was saying. "Don't give her any lectures because, God knows, there's nothing that turns a drunk away faster than a lecture. But just let her know that you know the real reason she didn't come."

Sam and Michael looked at each other. They had shrunk from that confrontation for so long.

"I know it's a hard thing to do," said the priest. "I'm sure she's convinced herself that you two don't know she's an alcoholic. She probably doesn't even admit she's an alcoholic. That's where I come in. I somehow have to convince her that the liquor is controlling her now and not the other way around."

"Are you scared of confronting another alcoholic?" Sam asked.

The priest smiled. "She's not my mother," he said gently. "No, I'm always hopeful. Down inside her, I believe there's a good whole person begging to get out. That's what I go looking for." He stood up. "I'll go see her in the next couple of days. But don't expect any miracles," he warned. "I may not get anywhere."

"At least somebody's going to try," Michael said as they went out into the street together. When Sam looked back from the top of the street, Father Fitzgerald was disappearing into the church.

"I'm not sure anything's going to happen," Father Fitzgerald reported to them a couple of days later. "But I tried."

"What did she say?" Michael asked.

"I'll spare you the details," the priest said with a wry smile. "Your mother is a smart woman, and like all cornered animals, she lashes out. She knows how to hurt. But then alcoholics are good at that. They can find your weak spots. The one time I felt a glimmer of hope was when I talked about the play. I think she did really want to come see it. It was the one concrete example I could give her that showed she was no longer in control."

"Did you tell her about the meetings?" Sam asked.

The priest nodded. "Don't be surprised if nothing happens," he said gently. "She still doesn't admit she's an alcoholic, and that's the first step. Until she admits that, nothing is going to change."

15

The record of her abuses became their daily diary.

September 29th. You dropped the teakettle when you were trying to pour hot water into a cup. It splashed all over Michael's pants. You swore at him for being so clumsy.

October 1st. A strange man came to the house and dropped off your wallet. He said he found it in the street. You didn't seem to know you lost it.

October 3d. You don't seem to care anymore about hiding the bottles. This afternoon when Sam came in from school, you and Mary Chadwick were drinking and listening to music down in the front room. The record player was turned on so loud that you didn't even hear the front door close.

October 4th. Uncle Theodore called and said he had been trying to reach you for two days but nobody answered the phone.

When we got home from school today, you were wandering around in just your slip but you didn't seem to notice or care that we saw you like that.

"I feel as if we're living with a devil or a whore or worse," Sam told Kathleen. They had gone back to meeting after school, either on his corner or down in the coffee shop. Ever since the play, things had changed between them. There was an easy closeness that had never been there before. "It's because we worked so well together," Kathleen told herself but she knew there was more to it than that. Sam didn't think anymore about her being older. He had begun to see her as separate from Michael and the rest of the family, separate from the memories of Pa and the dark front rooms of his house where he used to see them bent over books together. He wanted her all to himself.

"Your mother sounds as if she's going crazy," Kathleen answered quietly.

"I wish we could leave her," he said. "I feel trapped by that house and the memories of Pa and the weird way she's making it all seem—" He stopped. "—Seem dirty," he finished in a whisper. "She's rubbing our faces in her ugliness. I'll never be able to love her again."

"You might be able to love her," Kathleen said. "But you'll find it much harder to like her. I love my father still in a sort of pitying way, but I can't ever just talk to him comfortably. I hate it when we're in a room alone together."

"Don't you ever want to run away?" Sam asked.

She smiled. "I ran away across the street to your house almost every day for two years. Now I run away to college."

"Michael was saying we should move in with Uncle Theodore." Sam shrugged. "But that's no answer. That's just another kind of prison."

"If you really did pack up and leave, it might shake her up a bit," Kathleen said slowly.

"She would probably heave a sigh of relief and bring

out another bottle," Sam muttered. "Come on, let's go for a walk." They paid the bill and went out into the cool air.

They took the long way home. It wasn't a very pretty walk but it meant they could both put off facing whatever was waiting for them at home.

"Fall's here," Kathleen said, buttoning up her coat. She hated the cold weather. It seemed to close in on them for so long. There would be snow on the ground in another month.

"It's already been seven months since Pa died," Sam said. "Some days it seems like forever and other times I feel as if I just saw him yesterday. You know what I miss the most? The laughing. It seems to me that nobody's laughed in our house in months."

She smiled at him and he reached out and took her hand. "Your father did know how to laugh at himself," she said quietly. "It was one of his best qualities." They walked home in silence.

"I was thinking I might try to talk to your mother," Kathleen said as he turned to go in the house. "Do you think it would do any good? I am another woman, and I've been through it all with my father."

He didn't say anything for a minute. The way she talked about herself as a woman had distracted him. "I don't want her to hurt you," he said slowly after a long pause. "You haven't seen her lately. She can be so nasty." But he wasn't saying no.

"I'll think about it," Kathleen said.

"Why did you cut your hair?" he asked.

"I told you already. It's easier this way." She blushed without wanting to.

"I thought it was prettier the other way," he said, reaching up to push it back from her face.

"Sam," she said, embarrassed that they were standing

out on the sidewalk. She was sure Peggy was watching from their front stoop.

"See you tomorrow?"

"Yes," she said as she turned away.

"Kathleen," he called to her.

She turned back.

"If we weren't standing on Winthrop Street, I'd kiss you good-bye," he said with a smile.

She turned and ran toward her house. When he said things like that, she never knew how to answer.

When she got home, her mother was in the kitchen. She looked up from her place by the stove.

"You're late again tonight," she said in a tired voice.

Kathleen didn't answer. She poured herself a glass of milk and slipped into a seat at the kitchen table. It had been a long time since they had really talked to one another. Her mother looked at her curiously but didn't say anything. They both knew how easily they could start an argument and neither one of them wanted to.

"You look tired, Mummy. Why don't you sit down and let me stir that."

"That would be nice. I am tired today." She gave Kathleen the spoon and lowered herself into a seat.

She looks thin, Kathleen thought. I haven't really noticed lately. And so much older.

"How's that school?" her mother asked, looking down at her hands.

"Fine," Kathleen answered quickly. She didn't want to talk about school. There wasn't much time that they could be alone. The other kids would all be coming in soon for dinner.

"Tell me something, Mother. How do you know when you really care about a person?" That wasn't exactly what she meant.

Her mother glanced up at her. She shrugged. "It's hard to say. You just feel differently."

"Did you feel that way about Dad?"

"I don't think I remember," she said, a bitter tone creeping into her voice. "It was a long time ago, and so much has happened since." There was a pause. "No," she said softly. "I do remember. With him, there was a kind of tingle that I didn't feel with anyone else. He used to come by after work, and I remember waiting for him all day." She blushed. "Seems kind of silly now, when I think about it."

"Oh no, I don't think it's silly." She lowered the heat under the pot and sat down across from her mother.

"It's that Everett boy, isn't it, Kathleen?" She didn't answer. "Why can't you find a nice Irish boy? Someone from your own kind of people?" She was pleading now and Kathleen was surprised to see tears in her eyes when she looked up.

"Don't worry, Mother," she said softly. "I'm not going to run off and get married or anything. It's just that Sam and I used to be friends, and now it's more than that." She looked down at the table. "It's a funny, scary sort of feeling," she said softly. "Not being in control of things anymore, not in control of the way I feel." She could see her mother looking at her, and she knew she didn't understand. In her world, you fell in love and got married and had children. There was no other way to be. There were no other choices.

Kathleen stood up. "I should go study," she said quickly as she gathered up her books.

"Don't go getting yourself in trouble, girl," her mother said, the sharp edge back in her voice.

"I won't," Kathleen said as she escaped up the stairs.

She shut her bedroom door quietly behind her. She

walked over to the window and looked down at the street.

Why did she feel so confused about everything? Always before she had seen what she wanted and gone after it, but now she didn't know what she wanted. She knew that she cared more for Sam than for any other boy, but she didn't know how far it was going to take her. There were so many feelings fighting inside her. She wanted to escape from Charlestown and the old-fashioned ideas and rituals that trapped her. But at the same time, there was a security here that she couldn't quite let go of.

She glanced over at Sam's house. The lights were on in his room and in his mother's room on the second floor. She remembered the first time she'd gone to the house. When the word got around that Mrs. Everett was looking for a baby-sitter, Kathleen had gotten up her courage to apply for the job.

"But you barely look older than Sam," Mrs. Everett had said. "How old are you?"

"I'm thirteen. And I am the oldest in a large family, so I have had a lot of experience with children." Kathleen knew she sounded braver than she felt. The chair she sat on so carefully was covered in deep red velvet, and when she let her fingers slip down to touch it, she was shocked by its smoothness. All around the walls, dark serious faces looked down at her from their stiff portraits. Kathleen felt as if she were sitting in a museum. But she remembered thinking that Mrs. Everett had seemed nervous and out of place too.

"Well, I'll try you out, Kathleen. Come Sunday about eleven."

It was only after a few months in the house that Kathleen had the nerve to come when she wasn't really needed for baby-sitting. Mrs. Everett didn't seem to care and Dr. Everett encouraged her, amused by all the questions that she kept asking about the people in those portraits and the books and the furniture.

Kathleen lay back in her bed and closed her eyes. She missed him too and sometimes she wondered whether she hadn't fallen in love with him. It was the same kind of shiver that came over her now when she thought about Sam, about a certain way he looked at her or the nervous way he had of pushing his hair back off his forehead or his funny smile that often looked lopsided. She hated the trap he was in, the prison that house had become for him. She hated too the way the memory of his father was being violated by the strange demon that possessed his mother. "I am going to talk to her," she said out loud, hoping to be convinced by the sound of her own words.

16

When Kathleen rang the doorbell, she heard its sharp sound echoing away up the stairs. She had glanced at the bedroom windows when she crossed the street. The shades were pulled down.

"I know she's up there," Kathleen whispered to herself as she rang the bell again. Her hands were shaking but she pushed away the urge to turn and run down the street. She knew that if she didn't go through with this now, she would never get this far again. She heard someone fumbling with the lock on the inner door.

Mrs. Everett's face appeared suddenly, before Kathleen was ready for it. She was trying to button her blouse with one hand, and she peered at Kathleen for a long moment, as if trying to place her. Kathleen stared back, horrified by the changes in the woman's face. Mrs. Everett looked old and drawn and the skin under her eyes seemed to sag. Her hair had not been washed in a long time, and it stuck out from behind her ears in stiff wisps. Her eyes were glazed, and she blinked in the light like a baby waking up from a deep sleep.

"Kathleen?" she finally said. "What are you doing here?"

"I want to talk to you," she answered, her voice fainter than she meant it to be.

"Sam isn't home from school yet." She looked puzzled. "I'm sure he isn't. The alarm hasn't gone off." Kathleen pushed the door open a little wider and slipped inside. In the dark front hall, she could smell the liquor. She started up the stairs, scared that Mrs. Everett would make her leave unless she did something quickly. "I'll make you some coffee," she said loudly, glancing into the first-floor rooms as she climbed past them. Nothing had been moved and the furniture looked dusty and unused.

The older woman had closed the door and was quietly following her up the stairs. At least she hasn't thrown me out yet, Kathleen thought as she went into the kitchen. She put the kettle on to boil and wiped off the table with a sponge. Mrs. Everett had gone down the hall to her room. Kathleen could hear her opening a bureau drawer and closing it again sharply. She set two coffee cups out on the table and went through the cabinets until she found the instant coffee. As she was pouring the hot water, she heard Mrs. Everett coming back down the hall. She stood in the kitchen doorway watching. Kathleen finally looked up.

"I made some coffee," she said, slipping into a seat.

"What do you want?" Her face seemed clearer now and her voice was sharp.

"I want to talk to you. Would you like some coffee?"

"No." But she sat down in the other chair.

There was a short silence. Kathleen took a sip of the coffee. It was too hot, and she put the cup down quickly. She wasn't sure how to begin. But Mrs. Everett spoke first.

"If you've come to preach to me like your precious priest, you might as well leave now. I don't need all you people telling me how to run my life. I've had enough of it from my own family."

"Sam and Michael are worried about you," Kathleen said.

"Ha." The woman's eyes narrowed and she looked closely at Kathleen. "That's a lie. They're just hoping I'll go away somewhere and leave them alone."

She was right and Kathleen knew it.

"That's all their father wanted, too. Ever since I came up here people have been trying to get rid of me. Well, maybe I will go. See where that leaves them."

"You look thin," Kathleen said timidly. "It's not doing you any good to hide yourself away like this."

"What do you know about my life?" Mrs. Everett asked, tipping her head to one side in a strangely coy way. "Have you been watching me from your window, too? Don't think I don't know what goes on. He used to spy on me. He read my letters and hid things from me. And that mother of his. She was the worst. Always prying and poking. 'Deborah, have you taken the boys to see their aunt?' 'Deborah, don't you think Sam needs to wear a hat in this weather?' 'Deborah—'" She went on, her voice rising and falling steadily, her head jerking back and forth. She had slipped off into her own world, peopled with her own private demons. She's forgotten I'm here, Kathleen thought, watching the woman's face. She must recite all these things to herself over and over again. Every alcoholic needs his own excuses, Father Fitzgerald had once told her. The whole world's against them. That's why they drink.

Suddenly the voice stopped. Her eyes were on Kathleen again.

"Don't you want to stop drinking?" Kathleen asked

suddenly. "Can't you see how it's ruining everything for Sam and Michael? They need you now. They miss you." She spoke quickly, her words rushing out before she could stop them. She realized later that, in that moment, she had been pleading with her own father too. She was saying all the things to Mrs. Everett that she had always wanted to say to her father. "It must be horrible to be all alone but the drinking is just going to make it worse." The dark eyes across the table seemed to have softened, and suddenly Kathleen saw a yearning in them. She wants to stop, Kathleen thought. "It's because you have a disease. You're an alcoholic because—" But she never finished the sentence because the woman's hand whipped out across the table and slapped her face so hard that she couldn't speak. Mrs. Everett stood up and crept around the table. Her body was coiled up and she was speaking in a low, threatening voice. For the first time, Kathleen was really scared.

"You little bitch. Don't you call me an alcoholic." She grabbed Kathleen's arm and pulled her out of the chair. "You don't know what the hell you're talking about. I know what's been going on upstairs all these months. I've heard you going up those stairs with my son."

Kathleen pulled away in horror and backed out of the room.

"Do you know who you are talking to?" The woman's voice had risen to a shriek. "I am a lady, a southern-bred lady. I may not be your swish Boston aristocrat, but I know my manners. I know how to talk to people and I know how to drink." She burst into a crazy high-pitched laughter that ended abruptly. "If my mother ever heard you call me that name, she would take down your pants and spank your—"

"Shut up," Kathleen shouted, her voice filling the room. "Shut up." She covered her ears and ran down the stairs away from the wildly grinning figure. The last thing she heard before she closed the front door was the loud ringing of an alarm clock.

"It was all my fault," Sam said again. "I should never have let you go."

"I did it on my own," said Kathleen, her voice coming in jerks. She couldn't seem to stop crying. It had started the moment Sam came into her room. She was sure he would come in the house this time, and even Peggy had let him up without a word.

He opened the door and came right over to where she was sitting on the bed.

"Did she hit you?" he asked, pushing her hair away from her face. And she had shrugged as if to say it was nothing but, at that moment, she had started to cry. He pulled her up and put his arms around her. She leaned against him, soothed by the prickly roughness of his sweater and the rocking motion. She knew that the door was open behind him but she didn't care. She slipped her arms around his waist and they held each other for a long time without saying anything. Then he pulled away and looked at her.

"She must have said some horrible things to you," he said gently. "I'm sorry. I don't know what else to tell you. Except it's not really my mother we're dealing with."

"What are you going to do?" Kathleen asked, wiping her face with the back of her hand.

"I have an idea. I want to talk to Michael. If this doesn't work, I think we'll move out. Go to Uncle Theodore's." He smiled at her. "Thank you for trying. I shouldn't have let you do what I've been too scared to face." He leaned over and kissed her. She looked up and he was gone.

When Michael heard the story, he was amazed. "Kathleen's really got guts," he said. "Can you imagine one of us going in to her father and telling him to stop drinking?"

"We've been real cowards," Sam said. "What she did showed me that." He felt strangely calm about the confrontation that he knew they were going to have with his mother. It was an odd feeling after all the months he had spent running away from it.

"You think we should just read her the list?" Michael asked.

"That's right. No emotions, no impressions, just the facts. On such and such a day, you did such and such. From what Kathleen said, Ma still doesn't admit she's an alcoholic. Maybe all our facts will show it to her."

"She's going to get very angry," Michael said.

"That's why we both have to do it. As soon as she turns on one of us, the other one starts reading." Sam felt impatient with Michael. It was unlike him to sound so cautious.

"Well, we can't do it tonight," Michael said, getting up to go into his room. "She's locked in her room again."

"But you'll do it with me as soon as we get the chance?" Sam asked.

Michael grinned at him. "You really sound like my older brother these days." He nodded. "All right, fearless leader, I'll follow you unto the death." He raised an arm in mock salute and marched out of the room.

"Always the actor," Sam said to the empty doorway. He was thinking that six months ago Michael's parting would have irritated him. Now it made him laugh. So many things had changed.

The right time came later in the week. Ma had gone downtown to meet with Uncle Theodore and the ac-

149

countant. By the time Sam and Michael got home from school, her eyes looked glazed but she was dressed and making dinner in the kitchen. Sam signaled to Michael, and they went upstairs together.

"I'm more nervous than on opening night," Michael said in a low voice. "Why am I so scared of her?"

"Because she's unpredictable. Do you have the list?" Sam followed him into his room. "I almost wish she had drunk a little more," he said. "She can pull rank on us when she's sober. Her head is much clearer. All right, let's go."

She glanced up at them as they walked into the kitchen.

"Dinner's not quite ready yet," she said. "I'll call you."

"We want to talk to you, Ma," said Sam. He was proud of how steady his voice sounded. "Could you sit down, please?"

Michael pushed the list over to Sam, who took it with a glare.

"We want to read you something," said Sam, smoothing the worn paper with his hands.

Ma seemed to relax a little. She turned the heat down under the two saucepans and sat across the table from them.

Sam began at the beginning, reading in slow, sharp tones the list of her abuses. Michael sat close to his brother, watching Ma. At first, she looked composed, her face set in the same listening expression that used to come over her when he read his homework to her. But slowly her face changed as she realized what they were doing. Her eyes narrowed, and she opened her mouth once as if to say something. But then she closed it and leaned closer as if to hear better. Sam kept reading:

At Christmas lunch at Grandma's house, the
winter before Pa got sick, Michael saw you adding

something to your ginger ale. You were standing in the coat closet with your back to him and when you heard his footsteps, you turned and shouted at him to stop following you.

That same afternoon, Pa made you stop the car on the way home. He had to drive the rest of the way.

"It doesn't affect my driving, it never has," she whispered, more to herself than to the boys. Michael took the list from Sam and flipped ahead to the summer accident.

On June 21st, you had an accident on our way home from the summer trip. You refused to drive anymore, and Sam had to drive home from the expressway. He didn't have a license.

"I tried so damn hard," she exploded, her voice a violent noise in the room. "All that month, I kept taking it out and putting it away again. But you didn't want to help. You two acted like I didn't exist."

Sam nudged Michael to go on reading. They couldn't begin to argue with her. They had to get through the list.

After Pa got sick, there was only one time until he died. He moved out of the room into the TV room, and you didn't come out of the bedroom for three days. He used to give us money to do the shopping, and we had hamburgers every night. When we asked, he said you were sick.

She laughed, a jangling noise that sounded more like crying. "I was sick," she said slowly. "When I threw up that morning, he just told me to pull myself together. To your father, you had to be dying to be sick." There was a silence. Michael looked down at the table. "He wasn't an easy man to live with, Sam," she said in a low, pleading voice.

Sam shut his eyes. "Go on, Michael," he said.

Michael began to read about the summer. The dates got closer together and the incidents even more detailed. She shook her head from time to time as if confused by something.

"I don't remember that," she said once, and Michael stopped to glance at her.

"It happened, Ma," he said gently. "All these things happened." His voice sounded funny, a little weak. Sam took the list from him and finished it. The last entry was Monday, the day Kathleen had come. Sam had imagined Ma would explode again at that, but she said nothing. Her eyes were closed and she was pressing her temples roughly with her two index fingers as if to push some pain away. Michael got up and turned off the two burners.

There was a long silence. The house creaked as the November wind blew through the upstairs windows. The kitchen was growing darker, but nobody moved to turn on a light. Sam didn't even dare look at Michael. There was some spell over them that he felt she had to break. The charges had been read. Now they must be answered.

She sighed, a long, aching sound, and took her hands away from her face.

"Why do you hate me so much?" she asked, looking at Sam again. "Why did you always love him and hate me?"

Sam shook his head. "I didn't hate you, Ma," he whispered. "I never hated you—" But the way he broke off the sentence, they all knew there was more to say.

She stood up suddenly and went out of the room. Michael glanced at Sam and raised his eyebrows. They didn't dare speak because they were both sure she could still hear them.

She came back and sat down again.

"Did you go for a drink?" Michael asked suddenly.

She stared at him without answering.

"Ma, the alcohol is controlling you now," Michael started. "That's why we decided to read you this list. When you're in the middle of something like this, it must be hard to know what's happening to you. We wanted to show you."

"What do you know about it?" she asked sharply, her eyes glittering.

"Nothing," he said quickly. "I can only see what it's doing to you. And I hate the person it's making you. Sam and I miss you, Ma. The real you. We keep remembering you up at Maine, painting on the porch and walking with Pa in the woods. We want you to just come back to yourself again."

She was crying. There was no sound, but in the dim light they could see her shoulders shaking. Sam reached over and took her hand. Her skin felt cold but she did not pull away.

"I've been all alone," she whispered. "Ever since I came up here, I've been alone."

"We're here, Ma," Sam said. He started to say more but he couldn't.

She stood up again and looked at them closely. Sam looked down, scared to meet her eyes. He knew she would be able to see the fear and the disgust in his face. She smelled of bourbon, and her face looked drawn and old. Michael looked right back at her, his eyes steady.

"I'll try," she whispered to Michael. Then she went out of the room. This time they heard her door close.

"That's it," Sam said. "We won't get another chance."

Michael turned on the overhead light and lit the

burners again. They stared at each other in the cold, bright light.

"I'm exhausted," said Sam, putting his forehead down on the table.

"We said more to Ma in the last hour than we ever have before," Michael said. "I kept hoping Pa's ghost was hovering up there somewhere."

Sam had been thinking of Pa too. "Michael, I want to ask you something."

"Just a minute," he said as he dished their dinner into two plates. He sat down. "Okay, shoot."

"That last day when you went to the hospital—"

"Oh, no, Sam, don't bring that up again."

Sam shook his head. "I just want to know." He stopped. Michael was still eating. "What did he look like?"

Michael didn't answer for a long time. Finally he put down his fork. "He looked dead," he whispered, looking up at his brother. "His eyes were open but he couldn't see anything. He didn't know I was there. I touched his hand, and it felt cold and limp. There were so many things that I had come to say but he couldn't hear me." Michael closed his eyes. "I said them anyway."

"Said what?" Sam asked gently.

"How sorry I was that we had spent our whole lives missing each other. Passing like ships in the night, as Father Fitzgerald would say." Michael opened his eyes and looked down at his plate again.

"That's the way you and I used to be." Sam grinned.

"I know." A funny shiver passed through Michael. "I read something to him. Maybe he could hear it. It was something Father Fitzgerald once told me. An Irish blessing. Do you want to hear it?"

Sam nodded.

"'May the road rise to meet you. May the wind be

always at your back. May the sun shine warm upon your face, the rain fall soft upon your fields. And until we meet again, may God hold you in the palm of His hand.'" When Michael stopped, he was crying. "That's where I hope Pa is right now," he said in a cracked voice. "'In the palm of God's hand'."

Sam leaned over and patted his brother on the shoulder. It was a clumsy gesture but he didn't trust his voice enough at that moment to say anything.

17

Dear Sam and Michael,

I am going to tell you a lot of things in this letter
that I would never dare say to your faces. A lot of
things about myself and your father and the two of
you. I will probably surprise you and even shock you
but in a family where nobody has talked to each
other about the important things for so long, surprise is the least we can expect.

First of all, I'm going away for a while. I'm going
back to Savannah, where I haven't been since I
married your father. I need to get away from
Charlestown and all the good and bad memories of
the last few years. I know it will seem to you like I'm
running away from my problems, but it is just for a
while. I will come back, and I will be in better shape.
In the meantime, I realize from what you both told
me last night that you two can take care of yourselves. I have known that all along, and that's almost
what saddens me the most. Your father doesn't need
me anymore, and you boys don't really need me

either. I'm going to have to learn to live just for myself. I guess, right now, I'm the one who needs me the most.

"It makes me sad that she thinks that," Michael said. "We may not need her to cook our hamburgers or put on our snowsuits anymore, but we need her in other ways."

"We need a mother," Sam said simply. "I wish she realized that."

"I guess we have to tell her," Michael said. "Keep reading."

I want to tell you something about the way I grew up and about the marriage your father and I had. I have a history too, but it has been overwhelmed by the Everetts and their history. I am bitter about that, and I think I have a right to be. You know that I grew up in Savannah and that I was an only child. But you don't know how different it was from the life your father knew. My father was a doctor too, and although he loved his work, he was not consumed by it. He came home every night for dinner, and the three of us would sit down at the table and really talk. My mother was a shy woman, proud of us, truly happy with her life as a wife and mother and that was what she brought me up to be. There is a picture of her and my father in my bureau drawer. Go and look at it sometime.

"I remember it," Sam said. "She used to have it up on top of the bureau."

Every night my father would ask me how school was and what I had done in class and whether I had painted a new picture. He was genuinely interested. When I came up to Boston and met the noisy, self-centered, brilliant, argumentative Everetts, I was terrified of them. So, of course, I never said a word. I was used to being drawn out. I could never stand up at that big round table at your grandmother's house and shout out my accomplishments. All I could do was sit and listen. Your grandmother did try to bring me out. But even her way of asking me about my painting or you children seemed patronizing. As if it was a duty she felt bound to perform and as if she didn't really expect to hear anything interesting. As I read that over, I know it sounds small and whiny—

"It does," Michael said.

—but I am trying to put down here what I really felt.

You must be wondering why I married your father in the first place. Well, when I first met him, he was different from the others in the family. His voice was quiet and he had this intense look when he listened to me that was flattering and, I must admit, a little scary. We saw each other alone for a long time. I had known him for a year before I ever met his family. And by that time, I had accepted his proposal. I wonder now if he didn't do that on purpose—as if he knew they might scare me off.

After we were married and had moved to Beacon Hill, things were still good between us when we were alone. He encouraged me to paint as much as possible, and he took my work seriously as if it was more than just a hobby. But he began to get frustrated with my shyness when we went out to dinner or to the big house. He always left my side very quickly when we were in a group of people as if he was nervous about what I might say. It was almost as if he was embarrassed by me. I tried to talk to him about it a couple of times, tried to explain

158

why I acted the way I did. He listened, but I don't think he heard. You know how his attitude about many things was puritanical—buckle your boots, face the music. Slowly I discovered it was a lot easier to face the music with a glass of bourbon in my hand. I was funny and talkative, and he seemed pleased by the change.

"I feel as if we are listening to someone talking in front of the meeting down at the church," Michael said, leaning back in his chair. "If you close your eyes, she could be there right in front of us."

Sam nodded impatiently. He wanted to keep reading. He felt as if, at last, a lot of his questions were being answered.

Then you boys were born and I didn't have the time to paint anymore. You came closer together than we had really planned but we were both pleased because I had trouble getting pregnant. I was frustrated by motherhood. You seemed to take so much time and often your father would come home to chaos and he seemed irritated by my disorganization. For a while, we had a nurse that your grandmother hired for me, but that was even worse. She was very outspoken and confident and she wanted just to take over. But I didn't want to give you up completely. So I got up my nerve and fired her, and we returned to the former chaos, combined with the very obvious disapproval of your grandmother. I just was not the daughter-in-law she had envisioned for her only son. And once again I discovered that my late afternoon exhaustion was easier to deal with if I just had a little drink instead of a cup of tea. I knew your father wouldn't approve, so I was always sure to have it put away by the time he got home.

Then when you were twelve, Sam, we moved to Charlestown. I felt two ways about that. Much as I hated the social life of Beacon Hill and the way Grandmother Everett could keep an eye on me, Charlestown seemed a drastic solution. I would have loved to have gone farther out of the city, but your father was determined to move there. He loved the history of the place, I guess, and the excitement of doing something that he knew would shock his mother and sisters. He was always a rebel although his rebellions were small, private ones. When he sensed my reluctance about coming he just took the matter out of my hands. He bought the house and worked on it all by himself. I'm sure he was scared to show it to me. I did love the house when we first came here, but I felt more isolated than ever. The few friends I had were in Cambridge or Boston, and slowly I began to lose touch with them because it seemed such an effort to see them.

I lived for our summers up at the Point. I know you boys must have sensed some release of tension when we got there. I could paint all I wanted, and I felt happy and free. Your father responded to my relief. It was as if we all changed for the better. Sam, I remember you wishing we could live up there all the time, and I know what you meant.

I am sober now. I have not had anything to drink since I left the kitchen in the middle of our talk. I am glad you both finally said something to me. It must have been a hard thing to do. I know I have a problem, but I'm also sure I can beat it on my own. If I'm just given a little space, a little time to myself. I am going down to stay with a cousin of my mother's. She will be surprised to see me because I have not

written to her in a long time, but I know she will take
me in. The address is on the envelope.

I haven't put down here everything that I meant
to say. Maybe I will write you from down there after
I have thought everything through a little more. I
feel confused and very tired. If you need anything, I
know Holly and Theodore will help you. I have
written them a note telling them what I am doing. I
also told them not to worry about the two of you.
You can take care of yourselves and the house. They
will probably try to get you to move over with them,
but if you want to stay in Charlestown it is fine with
me.

I love you,
Ma

Sam tossed the sheets of paper on the table and got up. He walked up and down for a while before he remembered the orange juice he meant to pour for himself.

"Want some?" he asked.

Michael nodded. "What do you think?"

"I think she's kidding herself," Sam said quietly. "She'll never be able to stop completely by herself."

"I agree. It might even be worse, now that she's away from the few people who can talk to her honestly about it. Sit down, you make me nervous."

But Sam kept walking. "I'll be honest, I don't want her to come back right now. I'm glad she's gone. I feel as if some curse or spell has been lifted from the place."

"There are still a lot of things I would love to know," Michael said slowly, tapping a fork on the edge of the table. "I wonder how Pa really handled the drinking with her. Did he try to get her some help or did he just ignore it?"

"I'm sure he just closed his eyes and prayed it would go away," Sam said. "Isn't that the way he handled any kind of emotional problem?"

Michael glanced up at his brother. "I never expected to hear you say something like that."

"I didn't ever expect to say it," Sam admitted.

After breakfast they cleaned up the kitchen and went upstairs to get their books. Ma's bedroom door was open, and her bed was made. It felt strange to be in the house without her.

The third floor felt cold.

"We'll have to stuff the windows soon," Sam said. "Pa used to do it in October. I bet it snows any day now."

Michael opened the door to the storage room and went in. This part of the house was unheated, and they could see their breath in the air.

"This would be a perfect place for Ma to work," Michael said. "We should clear out all this junk and fix up the room for her. It might really inspire her."

"Let's wait and see what happens," Sam said. "She has to come back home first."

"You were right about talking to her," Michael said as he pulled the door shut behind him. "I feel this crazy sense of relief. At least we've done *something* after all this time."

Sam grinned. "For one night we forgot we were uptight Protestants. It's the same relief I felt that night we broke all the bottles."

"That seems years ago now," Michael said. "We've come a long way."

Sam nodded.

It took a lot of fast talking but Aunt Holly finally agreed to let them stay home.

"But I'm sending Jane over one day a week to clean the house, and I want you to come here for dinner at least twice a week." They were both listening on the same phone extension. Michael rolled his eyeballs at the receiver but Sam motioned to him to be quiet.

"Yes, Aunt Holly."

"And Uncle Theodore will take care of all the money matters."

"Yes, Aunt Holly."

There was a short silence. She finally seems to have run out of steam, Sam thought, and he started to say good-bye.

"Your poor mother, she must have really been desperate to run away like this."

"We were all pretty desperate," Sam said.

"What do you mean?" she asked.

Michael shook his head as if to say, don't bother trying to explain.

"Nothing," Sam said quickly. "Good-bye. We'll call you soon." And he hung up the phone very gently as if he were trying to turn off a radio without waking up somebody.

The letters from Ma came sporadically, sometimes two in one day and then nothing for weeks. It was hard to tell from what she said exactly how she was doing. There seemed to be no steady progression in one direction. And she never talked about coming home. She wrote mostly about the past as if she kept thinking of more she wanted them to know.

"It's as if she wants to be sure we know everything before she comes back," Michael said. "Make sure all the questions are answered so we won't bring up the ugly subject again."

"For all the talking she says she did with her father, she's just as scared of face-to-face meetings as the rest of us," Sam said.

"Oh, I guess everybody is," said Michael. "It certainly is hard to bare your soul to anyone."

"Sometimes."

One time, your father took the bottles out of the bar. I remember how surprised he was when he came home that night to find me drunk again. It was as if he didn't think I was old enough or smart enough to buy myself some more. He did treat me like a child much of the time. But then again, I often acted like one.

I would like to bring you both down here sometime. You must still be struggling through the knee-deep snow but yesterday it almost felt like spring here. I was outside for an hour with only a sweater on.

"I hate the way she always says *your* father as if he were no relation to her," Sam said.

"She's bitter," Michael said. "I don't blame her. The famous Everett family doesn't sound as if they were very understanding."

Your father's work meant so much to him. Sometimes I hated being left out just because I couldn't understand what he was doing. And he was so busy. Another conference, another paper to give, another special patient. If I had dropped dead, his life would have gone on much the same as before. I resented not feeling that important, that committed to something. I must sound selfish. That's what Aunt Lydia always said about me. Those two sisters fussed over their little brother so. I'm not a fusser. I guess you boys have always known that.

"I'm glad of it too," Sam said. "Can you imagine a mother worrying over you all the time?"

Michael grinned. "One stroke for Ma."

They wrote her back but their letters were not as open. It was easier to tell her news of the house or school. After a while, their sense of freedom passed, and they began to miss her. Sam brought it up first.

"I've begun to dread getting home at night," Sam said. "This house feels too big for just the two of us."

"Do you want her back?" Michael asked.

Sam didn't answer for a while. "I guess," he said slowly. "I want her back if things have really changed. I know I don't want to go through those scenes from last summer again."

They dropped in to see Father Fitzgerald.

"I'm glad you two came by," he said. "I'm planning a new play. Are you interested?"

"Are you crazy?" Michael asked. "Of course we are."

"Is it the one you've been working on with Kathleen?" Sam asked.

"Yes. Did she tell you about it?"

Sam nodded. "It's about the Irish immigration to Charlestown. Kathleen's done lots of research on it for a paper," he explained to Michael.

"And now we're turning it into a play," Father Fitzgerald said with a smile. "I never thought I'd try my hand at writing."

Michael didn't say anything. He was looking at the floor.

"Have you heard from your mother?"

"Yes," Sam said. "We're actually beginning to miss

her. The house seems so big and empty with just the two of us. But we're scared to have her come back too. The whole thing could start again, couldn't it?"

The priest nodded. "Very easily. Especially if she hasn't gotten help. If she's trying to kick the bottle by herself, she'll be even more vulnerable when she gets back and faces her old problems. Do you notice any real change in her letters?"

Sam and Michael glanced at each other. "Not really," Michael said. "She's pouring out a lot of her feelings about the past, but she hasn't told us much about what her life is like down there."

"Have you talked to her on the phone?"

"No."

"You might try calling her. You can tell more from her voice than letters."

"When are you going to start rehearsals on this play?" Michael asked suddenly.

Sam laughed. "You can see what he's thinking about."

"We have to finish writing it first," Father Fitzgerald said. He pointed to a pile of papers on the edge of his desk. "There it is. Do you want to read what we've got? You can take it home for a day or two if you want."

Michael started reading on the way up the hill. He went right up to his room when they got home and read the play through.

"How is it?" Sam asked when he heard him come out in the hall.

"Not bad," Michael said, handing it over. "I think Kathleen wrote most of it. It sounds more like her."

"You don't sound very enthusiastic," Sam said, watching his face.

"It's another Irish play. There are two male leads. Now, who do you think is going to get them? Patrick and Kevin." He shrugged. "I was thinking I might try to join

166

an acting group in Cambridge this summer. Mr. Macmillan was telling us about it in rehearsal the other day."

"Father Fitzgerald will be disappointed," Sam said.

"Well, he can't expect me to keep taking all the small parts just because I'm not Irish."

Sam nodded. "You're right."

Aunt Holly had called them every afternoon in the first weeks, but slowly she had accepted the fact that the two boys could take care of themselves. They still went there for dinner twice a week, and the four of them were beginning to relax with each other. The boys began to see a side of Uncle Theodore they had never known before, a teasing way he had with Aunt Holly that made her look down in her lap and blush.

"You know, I think they still love each other," Michael said one night on the way home.

"You sound surprised," Sam said.

"Well, aren't you? What other grown-ups can we say that about? Ma and Pa never acted that way toward each other except at the end. They always seemed to miss each other. You know what I mean. Their timing was off."

Sam nodded. "Ma would cook a special dinner, and Pa had to stay late at the hospital. Or the time Pa sent her flowers, and they never arrived."

"Pa wasn't the romantic type," Michael said slowly. "That must have been hard on her. I think she cared a lot about things like that."

Kathleen was working very hard at school, and days went by when Sam didn't see her at all. This frustrated him because he found himself thinking about her a lot. Sometimes he suspected that she was avoiding him. He brought the subject up one night when they were walking up the hill from the movies.

"Come to my house for a while," Sam said when they started down Winthrop Street.

"Where's Michael?" she asked as they climbed the stairs to the kitchen.

"He's at a rehearsal at school," Sam said, trying to make his voice sound matter-of-fact. He did not tell her Michael was spending the night at Aunt Holly's because the rehearsal wasn't letting out until late. She hesitated for a moment on the steps but followed him slowly into the kitchen.

"I can only stay a little while," she said, letting herself down into the seat. "Mum is expecting me home."

Sam didn't answer. He got out the bottle of wine he had bought that afternoon and opened it.

"What's this?" she said when he put the wine glasses down in front of her. "Some special celebration?"

"No," he said. "I just felt like doing something different tonight."

She took a sip of wine, watching him all the time.

"I don't see much of you anymore," he said slowly. "I feel as if you're avoiding me."

"I've got a lot of courses this term," she said.

"That sounds like an excuse," he said. She didn't answer.

They sat in silence for a long time, lost in their own thoughts. There was something more they both wanted to say but neither one of them knew how to start. In the end they spoke at the same time.

"You first," Sam said with a grin.

"You're right," she admitted. "I have been avoiding you a bit."

"Why?"

She shrugged. "I'm not sure how I feel about you. Or

what you really think of me." She was scared he would think she wanted some declaration of love. She didn't even know what she wanted to hear. He was looking down at the table so she couldn't see the expression on his face.

"You're the first girl I've ever gone out with." It was hard for him to admit that. He wanted her to think that he was very experienced, but she knew too much about him. "Imagine that, my little brother's baby-sitter." He laughed nervously. She didn't answer.

"Look, Kathleen, why be so dramatic and serious?" he said suddenly. "I like being with you. I like talking to you." He shrugged. "Can't we just leave it at that?"

She smiled. "But that's just what I wanted to say. We can still be friends."

He frowned. "Well, a little more than friends," he said taking her hand.

She nodded and raised her wine glass. "Here's to us. Two people who are a little more than friends." They drank to that. She leaned over the table and kissed him gently. "Thanks, Sam," she said, and then she was gone. When he heard the front door close, he let out a quiet whoop.

18

It was in early February that they noticed a change in Ma's letters. She began to talk about the future as if she believed she had one to look forward to.

You won't believe it. I went out yesterday and bought myself a drawing pad and some pencils. I sketched for an hour and although my fingers feel awkward and the results are terrible, I'm not scared of it anymore.

And the next day she wrote:

I've joined a group down at the church. It is probably like your priest's meetings where people stand up and talk about themselves. I wouldn't have gone by myself, I'll admit that. But about a month ago, I took a drink for the first time since I've been here, and two days later Margaret found me in a hospital. I don't know what happened. I don't remember any of it. That's what scared me more than anything. Margaret knew of this group down at her church and she took me.

You would like Margaret. She's a no-nonsense kind of person, and she says just what she thinks. Sometimes she can hurt you but I find her honesty refreshing. I never feel guilty around her because she would tell me if I were hurting her or making her angry.

"There's a message there," Michael said, putting the letter back in the envelope.

"Her guilt probably drove her back to the bottle faster than anything," Sam said thoughtfully. "That never occurred to me before. I remember reading in one of those books last summer that an alcoholic hates himself worse than anyone else."

The next weekend they dragged home some big cartons from the grocery store and began to clear out the storage room.

"I'm going to call Kathleen," Michael said soon after they started. "She would kill us if she knew we were throwing out all this stuff without telling her. You know how she loves this room."

"She said something about working on a paper in the library today," Sam said.

"You sure know her every movement," Michael remarked with a grin. "What's been happening between you two?"

"What do you mean?"

"You just seem awfully cozy these days," Michael said.

Sam didn't say anything. There were some things you didn't have to talk to a younger brother about, he decided.

"I'm going to try her anyway," Michael said going down the stairs.

She did come over. "This place is much better than any library," she told Sam with a shrug.

They spent the whole afternoon in the room, going through the battered toys and the pictures and the trunks of old clothes.

"What are you going to do with this room?" Kathleen asked as she sorted through a carton of books.

"Turn it into a studio for Ma," Michael said. "She wrote last week that she's begun to paint again. It would be a sort of homecoming present for her."

"You'll have to insulate it," Kathleen said. She was still wearing her jacket. "It's so cold you can see your breath in here."

"I know," Michael said. "We don't know how to do that."

"My uncle is a carpenter. He could probably do it for you."

"Really? Will you call him? We'd love to get it done before Ma comes home."

"How are we going to pay for it?" Sam asked.

"I bet Uncle Theodore will give us some money from the estate for it," Michael said. "He's not going to quibble about something like this. It can't cost that much anyway."

Sam wasn't listening. He had found a photo album he had never seen before.

"Look at this," he said eagerly. "I think it's Ma's family."

They gathered around him on the floor and peered at the brown-tinted pictures. They didn't recognize the handwriting, but they knew from the captions that it must be their grandmother's.

"Deborah's graduation from elementary school."

"Deborah trying on her father's hospital coat."

"Deborah at her friend Wendy's ninth birthday party."

"The family at the Easter outing."

"Deborah with Cousin Margaret."

That picture showed a pretty, dark-haired girl about ten years old holding the hand of a young woman.

"That must be who Ma is with now," Michael said, leaning closer to see her face. "She looks very prim and proper in this picture."

"Our grandmother was pretty," Sam said, pointing to a photograph of a small woman sitting on the front steps of a clapboard-sided house. She had a shy smile on her face, and she was holding onto a floppy hat that looked like it might blow off.

"It is incredible," Kathleen said suddenly, sitting back on her heels. "There's this whole world your mother knew that completely disappeared when she came up here. There wasn't anybody here she could talk to about it, was there? How lonely."

"She was really very brave to come," Michael said. "It would have been easier to stay at home with the people she had known all her life."

"The problem was that nobody in Pa's family was interested in her old life," Sam said slowly, flipping through the pages.

"I think the most amazing thing is to look at these people who were related to us and realize that we will never meet them," Michael said. He pointed to a picture of their grandparents. "If those two people had not existed we wouldn't be here either."

The other two said nothing, and they flipped through the rest of the pictures in silence.

"I'm getting cold," Kathleen said. "We'd better hurry and finish this."

In the end, they took four big cartons downstairs to the trash. Michael put together a box of clothes for the costume wardrobe down at the church, and they put the photo albums and some of the books on the empty shelves in Pa's room. Sam got out the vacuum cleaner and did the floor, and when he was finished, they stood in the doorway and admired their work.

"It's really a very big room," Kathleen said.

"Same size as the kitchen," said Michael.

"Where is Ma's easel?" Sam asked. "The one she used to put up on the porch at the Point? We could set it up for her."

They rummaged through the house until Michael found it in the closet in the downstairs dining room. Together they set it up in the corner of the room closest to the window.

"It does make the room look authentic," Kathleen said as she started down the stairs. "Can I leave my box of stuff here for a while? I have to go to the library now."

"Sure," Sam said. "What did you keep?"

"Books mostly. They must have been ones your father collected. The titles sound like him."

Michael picked up the box of clothes and headed out the door after Kathleen. "I'm going to take these down to the church," he called to Sam.

"Do you want some help?"

"No, thanks. I want to talk to Father Fitzgerald about something."

The box was heavier than he thought and he had to drag it the last half block. Father Fitzgerald heard him struggling with the door and came to help him.

"Michael, what's all this?"

"We cleaned out the storage room in our house to make a studio for Ma. I thought you could use the old clothes for the costume box."

"Great. Is your mother coming home?" the priest asked as together they carried the box across the stage.

"Well, she hasn't said that she's coming, but her letters sound much more positive. She says she joined a group for alcoholics and she started painting again."

After they put away the clothes, Michael followed the priest into his office.

"Did you get the play back?" he asked. "I dropped it off last week but you weren't here."

"Yes, thanks. What did you think of it?"

"It's pretty good. The characters are all very believable, and I think you've given a good picture of Charlestown." He leaned on the edge of a chair and watched the priest pour himself a cup of coffee.

"Do you want some?"

Michael shook his head. "You drink too much of that stuff," he said with a grin.

"Most ex-alcoholics become coffee addicts," Father Fitzgerald answered. "Good. I'm glad you like it. I think Patrick and Molly are both interested in doing it too, so I thought we'd start rehearsals in the spring."

Michael looked down at the floor. "I don't think I'll be joining you again," he said slowly. "My drama teacher at school told me about a summer acting group in Cambridge, and I've sent in an application."

"Oh dear, we aren't fancy enough for you anymore," the priest said with a short laugh. His voice sounded bitter.

"No, it's not that. It's just that it's another Irish play, and you always feel that Patrick and Kevin should have the lead parts. I don't blame you for that. I agree with what you're trying to do but I want to be an actor so I've got to try some other kinds of plays." The words came tumbling out very quickly. He wanted to say how sad he felt about his decision but he was silent.

"I hadn't thought of that before," the priest said. "You're right. It is time for you to branch out. It's just that we'll miss you." There was a pause. "I'll miss you."

"It won't be the same for me either," Michael said quietly. "But don't worry. I'll be down here to hound you. And I'm pretty sure Sam will work on the set again if you want him. Pa and Sam did a lot of research on Charlestown and the way it used to look."

"Good idea. I'll ask him," the priest said.

There didn't seem to be any more to say. Michael said good-bye and walked out slowly. When he looked back through the half open door, the priest was still watching him. They waved to each other.

"What are you acting so sad for?" Sam asked when Michael told him about it. "You're not moving away or anything."

"I don't know," Michael said. "I'm just sort of moving on in spirit, I guess. I'll miss seeing him every day."

"The way I missed Pa in the beginning," Sam said.

"Yes," Michael muttered as he went up to his room.

Kathleen's uncle came to the house the next weekend and insulated the studio room. Sam and Michael painted it and put some books up on the shelves.

"That's all we should do," Michael said. "She'll want to make her own place of it."

"It would be great to come home in the afternoons and find her working up here," Sam said slowly. He was looking out the window over the snow-covered rooftops. "But I'm scared to even think about it. All the horrors of last summer are still too close."

Michael came over and stood beside him at the window.

"Do you realize it will be a year next week that Pa died?" he said. "I can't believe how quickly it's gone."

"I still miss him. The feeling comes over me when I least expect it." Sam leaned his forehead against the cold pane. "But he is less of a person for me than he was in real life. For the first time, he really disappointed me. Funny, because it's usually the other way around. After a person dies, you are supposed to remember the good parts. I've spent this year getting to know Pa's weaknesses."

"It's unfair for him," Michael said. "He's not here to defend himself."

"I wish he were," Sam said as he turned away from the window. They went downstairs, pulling the door shut behind them.

19

Michael was the first one home that afternoon, and he knew she was there the moment he opened the front door. There was the vague smell of perfume in the front hall and a strange silence in the house as if somebody had just stopped what they were doing to listen. For one brief minute he wanted to go out again, to put off seeing her for a while, to compose his face so that the disappointment wouldn't show if he were going to be disappointed. But the moment passed, and he realized how much he did want to see her.

"Ma?" he called softly. He heard her footsteps in the hall, and he bounded up the stairs. They almost collided but he stopped himself just in time and threw his arms around her.

"Hello, Michael," she said shyly, succumbing to his bear hug. They had not hugged each other in a long time, not since he was a little boy.

"You should have told us you were coming. We would have cleaned up a little more," he said, waving his hand at the kitchen.

"That doesn't matter," she said. "I didn't even really know I was coming until I got on the bus."

"You look great, Ma," Michael said. Her skin had lost that drawn, gray look and her cheeks were red with a sunburn. She had on a new dress that fit her and showed that she had put on some weight.

"Where's Sam?"

"He should be home soon. We have a surprise for you. You haven't been upstairs, have you?"

"No. I was just unpacking."

"When Sam comes home, we'll show it to you."

She glanced up the stairs a little nervously. "Is it a new pet? Or a boarder?" she asked with a laugh.

"Don't start asking questions," he said, following her into her room. They were still in there talking when Sam closed the front door. They could hear him stopping to listen just as Michael had.

"Is he still angry with me?" Ma whispered to Michael.

He shook his head. "No, not anymore. We've missed you," he answered quietly.

"Hello, Sam," she called and went out to meet him. Michael didn't move.

Sam noticed immediately the change in his mother. He smiled and kissed her on the cheek.

"Welcome home, Ma," he said.

"I have to look up at you now," she said. "Have you really grown that much?"

Michael came out into the hall. "I was waiting until you got home to take her upstairs. Come on, Ma."

They marched solemnly up to the third floor. Michael pushed open the studio door and led her through without saying anything. She walked all around the room slowly, stopping to look out the window and touch her easel.

"It's your studio," Michael said eagerly. "The one Pa

always said he was going to build for you."

"It's cold in here but we had it insulated, and with a little electric heater, it should be all right in the winter," Sam explained.

She took a deep breath and shut her eyes for a minute. They could both see she was crying. "It's beautiful," she said with a shy smile. "My own room. I've never really had my own room to work in. But I've only just started painting. The pictures are terrible. It's like learning to walk again. The brush feels so clumsy."

Michael laughed. "Don't be crazy, Ma. We don't care what the pictures look like. Give yourself some time. You haven't painted in ages."

"Not since that last summer up at the point," she said slowly.

"We'll have to get out your sun hat," Sam said. "I can't imagine you standing at the easel without that hat."

They all laughed at the thought of her standing in the cold room with her summer hat on.

"And the window faces west, doesn't it?" she said. "For my sunsets."

There was a short silence. "Come on," she said at last. "Let's go out to dinner tonight. We'll splurge and go to that seafood place in Boston. I brought back some pictures of Savannah to show you, and I want to hear what's been happening at school."

Those next few weeks were tense for all of them. They were like blind people groping toward each other, sometimes touching, sometimes knocking clumsily into one another.

"Ma just told me she wanted to know which nights I have to stay late for rehearsals," Michael grumbled one morning on the way to school. "She's got to understand that we can take care of ourselves now."

"Be glad she cares," Sam said. "You can't have it both ways."

In the afternoons when the boys got home, they often found Ma upstairs in her studio. She had bought two huge posters and hung them on the two opposite walls. The pictures brightened up the room. "They make it really mine," Ma explained shyly. "Your father never liked abstract art."

For the first couple of weeks, it seemed she just sat there. The easel was not touched, and she did not open her paint box. She brought up an electric heater and a hot plate to make tea. "I'm settling in," she explained to Sam. "Getting used to the place."

"That's great, Ma," he said honestly. "That's what we wanted." She seemed calm and happy. But they were still waiting. When Michael had suggested going down for one of the meetings at the church, she refused.

"She didn't seem angry with me for bringing it up," Michael told Father Fitzgerald. "But she didn't want to discuss it either."

"Maybe she's really kicked it on her own," the priest said. "I've seen some people do it. But they didn't have a long history of alcoholism like your mother's. We'll just have to wait and see."

Sam had begun to take up photography again. In the afternoons, he came home to work in his darkroom on the third floor, and he and Ma would stop and talk to one another during their breaks. For the first time, Ma seemed interested in his pictures, and he showed her how the enlarger worked and what the different chemicals were used for.

"Okay," he said with a laugh as she started back to her room. "It's your turn. Can I see what you're working on?"

"All right," she said. "Come on in."

She showed him her sketchbooks. "I'm still just using the pencils," she admitted. "That paint box is too frightening." She had brought up some of the photo albums they had put away in Pa's office, and she was sketching the faces, small studies done with light gray strokes. Sam had never seen her work in that style before, and he commented on it.

"I'm not sure of my line yet," she said. "This is one of the exercises they used to give in school the first few weeks of the term."

"We found this book when we were cleaning out up here." Sam pointed to the album of her family. "Michael and I had never seen it before."

"I guess it got buried under the Everetts. Sort of like me." She smiled and, for once, her voice didn't sound bitter.

Sam stood up and went to the window. "Your letters told us a lot Michael and I never knew," he said slowly. "It must have been hard to come into this family. I'd never really thought about it before."

"I'd never really told anybody before." She smiled again. "Those letters were good for me too. I didn't even know how angry I was. I stored it up for a long time."

There was a silence. Sam started to go but she spoke again as he was crossing the room.

"It was my fault too, Sam. Margaret helped me to see that. I could have spoken up and told them how I was feeling, even if it meant shouting. I took the easier way out, hiding from everything." Her eyes looked bright. Sam thought she might cry. "When someone dies, you want to go back and change things. To take back words you said, to say things you should have. That's the worst part about being left behind."

"I learned a lot about Pa this year," Sam said. "He came down a few notches."

"Don't blame him," she said softly. "I don't ever want to change how you felt about him. What you shared with your father was very special."

"We left some people out," he said looking at her. They both knew what he meant. "I'm sorry," he said as he walked quickly out of the room.

"It's something about that house," Sam told Michael much later. "You walk in the front door and before you even put your foot on the first step, you can sense what the mood is upstairs."

"It's not the house," Michael said. "It's the people in it."

That particular afternoon, something had stopped Sam before he ran up the stairs. Some silence, some tension. "Ma?" he called but he knew already that she wouldn't answer. He knew before he got to the top of the steps that her bedroom door would be closed. He knew before he knocked that she wouldn't open the door.

He sat at the empty desk chair in Pa's office, arguing with himself. He wanted to go upstairs the same old way without saying anything. He wanted to run away but he knew he would hate himself for it later. He knew that then he would be no different from Pa. And he would have no right to criticize.

He went and knocked on the door again. She didn't say anything.

"Ma, it's Sam," he said. "Please open the door." There was a creak from the bedspring but no other sound. He would have to talk through the closed door. Well, maybe that would be easier.

"I know you must be drinking again. We're going to stop pretending it's not happening. It won't be as easy as it was last summer because Michael and I aren't going to leave you alone."

He stopped. He was trying to decide what to say next. He was sure she was really listening and it scared him. What he was saying suddenly seemed so important.

"Ma, you've got a disease. You need help to cure it just the way Pa needed those blood transfusions to live that extra year. You just can't do it by yourself. Nobody can."

"I don't need your help," she shouted suddenly.

"You're right," Sam said. "You need to talk to people who have the same disease. I don't have it. I don't know what it's like."

He heard Michael coming up the stairs behind him. They looked at each other, and Sam saw the same look of fear and anger cross his brother's face.

"You've got to say something to her," Sam whispered fiercely. "We can't hide from it or we'll go right back to last summer."

Michael pushed his arm away. "All right, all right. Just wait a minute." He stood outside the door in silence for a minute.

"Ma," he called. "It's Michael." He looked at Sam and shrugged sheepishly. Sam glared back.

Michael took a deep breath and started again. "Ma, we know you're drinking again. Please come out. Please don't start all over again." His voice broke, and he bolted upstairs without another word. Sam didn't try to stop him. He had said something. Next time it would be easier. As long as they were both honest with her, things would have to be different, he thought. But he couldn't tell if he was just trying to convince himself.

Sam went out and walked across to the Murphys' house. He hadn't seen Kathleen for a while.

Peggy answered the door. "Kathleen," she yelled over her shoulder. "There's someone here to see you."

Kathleen's face appeared at the top of the stairs. She smiled. "Hi, Sam."

"Come on out for a walk. It's a nice day. Almost feels like spring."

She hesitated. "I'm working on that play," she said.

"Oh, all right, just for a while. I'll get my coat."

"Haven't seen you in a while, Mister," Peggy said.

Sam laughed. She had a big mouth for a twelve-year-old.

"That's because it's too cold for you to hang out on the front stoop. The view must not be as good from the window."

Peggy turned away without answering and disappeared through the door to the kitchen.

"Your sister makes me laugh," Sam said as they turned the corner.

"She drives us all crazy," Kathleen said. "She's running around with some tough group of kids from the high school now and my mother's all fussed over her. But then my mother has to worry about something or she couldn't draw her first breath in the morning."

"Speaking of mothers," Sam said.

"I ran into yours last week at the butcher's. She looks fine."

"That was last week," Sam said dryly.

"Is she drinking again?"

"She started today. It's the first time since she's been back. Probably the first time in a couple of months." He put his arm around her. "But you would have been proud of me, old girl. I actually talked to her about it. Through a closed door, but I told her I knew she was drinking and it was a disease and she needed help to stop. I doubt it will make any difference to her, but it changes things for me."

"What do you mean?"

He thought for a minute without answering. "I don't hate her anymore. I guess I believe what I am saying.

Alcoholism is a disease, and she can't control it herself. All she can do is admit it and go to someone for help." He took a deep breath. "And because I've told her what I think I don't go around hating myself anymore either. I think I'll be able to go on with my life without thinking constantly about her."

Kathleen smiled at him. "You must feel free," she said quietly.

"I do. I feel better than I have since Pa died. As if I've put something behind me."

"I should try talking to my own father," Kathleen said softly.

"I hold you responsible," he said, stopping to look her in the eye. She waved him away. "No, really, if you hadn't gone to talk to her I might have let things go on that way forever."

They walked on for a while in silence. "It must be one of the hardest things to accept," Sam said slowly. "That your parents are just people too. With all the faults and all the good parts of other people."

"Come on. Let's think about something else." She took his hand and started to run. "I'll treat you to a piece of cake at the new bakery."

Sam got home soon after dark.

"She's gone out," Michael said, coming out of the kitchen. "I heard her door open, and I came downstairs when she was putting on her coat. She just looked at me sort of crazily and went out the front door."

They found out the next day where she had gone. Father Fitzgerald called that afternoon.

"Your mother came to our meeting last night," he told Sam.

"So maybe it did make a difference," Sam said more to himself.

"What?"

"Michael and I said something to her yesterday when we came home. We knew she had started again," Sam explained.

"Yes, she came quite drunk, but Ann got her to take some coffee. I don't know if she'll come again, but it's a start."

"Thanks for letting us know," Sam said and hung up.

Ma kept to herself the next couple of days. They let her alone, but the silence between the three of them was a comfortable one. She seemed to understand and appreciate the space they gave her.

"Ma reminds me of that clown Grandmother gave us for Christmas one year," Michael said to Sam.

Sam looked confused. "Which one?"

"The one with the weight in the bottom. If you kicked it over it would swing back and forth wildly and the swings would get shorter and finally it would right itself slowly."

"It always did right itself eventually," Sam said with a smile.

Sam noticed the spring coming this year. He realized that last year, after Pa died, whole months had gone by emptily. The last stubborn patches of ice finally melted away down the gutter and the first good rain washed the salt stain from the sidewalks. People came out of their houses on the first warm day, unwrapped and pale-faced, and greeted each other heartily. "If it snows again now, I'll die," Kathleen said. "Every year it tricks us. There's always that one last April storm."

"Not this year," Sam said confidently. "I don't feel it in my bones."

He was right. Spring just kept rolling in as if nothing would stop it. Sam and Kathleen met down by the

Charles some afternoons after school. The trees were red and feathery with new buds and even though the wind off the river was brisk and cold, the new leaves held and grew. Sam asked Ma to join them one afternoon, and she came with her sketchbook. She and Kathleen didn't say much to each other but they didn't seem to mind being together. Ma did a sketch of an old man and his dog. When she was finished, the man asked grumpily to see the picture. He nodded without saying anything and handed it back to her.

"Don't you think it's good?" Sam asked eagerly.

"Don't ask him that, Sam," Ma said.

"The dog's good," he growled at them before he walked away.

"They have the same walk," Kathleen said as they stood watching the old pair cross the grass.

Ma burst out laughing. "You're right. They're both bowlegged."

"Thanks for asking me to come along," she said to Sam after dinner. "I should get out of Charlestown more often."

Michael had been accepted in the Cambridge acting group for the summer session.

"What did Father Fitzgerald say?" Sam asked.

Michael grinned. "He asked me if you'd help out with the sets this summer."

"Kathleen mentioned that to me too. I'm not sure. I really wanted to concentrate on my photography and I'm taking those driving lessons. But I could probably do it."

"I'm already beginning to miss the Point again," Michael said. "I always get this feeling when the days get hot."

Sam agreed. He had been thinking the same thing the last few days. "I've got an idea. Did you see that sign Mr.

Treadwell posted on the bulletin board last week? He's renting his house in New Hampshire this summer. I thought maybe Ma could talk to him about renting it for a couple of weeks. It's on a lake, and there's a boat and lots of walking trails."

Ma liked the idea. "I have to admit I was getting depressed about staying in Charlestown all summer. But—" She didn't finish her thought.

"What's worrying you?" Sam asked.

"I don't know if I'll be ready. To go off on my own like that."

At first Sam didn't understand what she meant. "It's for the three of us," he said slowly, watching her face. "If we can get it in August, after Michael's finished with his group in Cambridge." But he could see from her expression that he hadn't understood what she meant.

She looked down at her hands. "To be away from the group for so long."

"Oh," he said. "I hadn't thought of that. You've been just fine. . . ."

Her eyes narrowed. "Do you know what I think about first thing every morning?"

He shook his head.

"A drink. When I wake up that's the first thing I want. Still. And I haven't had a drink in over two months." She was silent for a minute. "Ann says she feels that way too, and she hasn't had a drink for over a year."

Sam felt horrible, and he didn't know what he could say to her. He hadn't thought about what she'd been going through every day. He had just been enjoying the difference in her.

She smiled at the stricken look on his face. "Don't worry. I'll figure out a way. We'll get out of here for a while."

"Oh Ma, that's not what I'm worried about. I just realized I've already begun to take your soberness for granted."

"Don't ever do that, Sam. It will never be something we can just take for granted." She stood up quickly as if to push away the thought. "Let's go call Mr. Treadwell."

They took the house in August. It was only a cottage with two small bedrooms, but the front porch looked out over the lake to a wooded island where they took picnics. The path around the lake went by the shore, and they got used to the sound of voices floating clearly up to them as they sat on the porch eating dinner.

Sam took roll after roll of black and white film, concentrating on still-life pictures that he caught on his afternoon walks in the woods.

"It's not the point," Michael said. "But I like it here." He had done well in the Cambridge group, and he was pleased with himself. They had asked him to come back next summer and the director had promised him a lead in one of the two plays they were planning to put on.

Ma set up her easel on the front porch. "Where else?" she said with a smile when she saw Michael watching her from the front door. She worked there in the afternoons when the air was still, and the boys had gone down to swim or take out the boat. She soon used up all the canvas she had brought with her, and Sam offered to drive the twenty miles to an art supply store to buy her more. Michael went with him. When they got home, Ma was sitting stiffly in her chair. One hand was gripping the other so that her knuckles burst out tight and white from her thin tan hands.

"Where have you been?" she asked in a soft, tense voice. "Why were you gone so long?"

The two boys frowned at each other behind her back.

"We stopped for ice cream, Ma," Michael said. "What's wrong?"

She didn't answer. Her shoulders were shaking. Sam went around and stooped down in front of her. He was frightened by the desperate look in her face.

"I want a drink," she whispered to him, her mouth spitting out every word separately.

"Oh, no," Sam heard Michael say. Sam knew she was counting on him to do something to stop her.

"Where's the bottle?" he asked sharply. "Where did you hide it?"

Her eyes kept staring at him but her gaze was going blank. He glanced up at Michael. "Go call Father Fitzgerald," he said. "Ma wants to talk to him."

"I do not," Ma said, but her protest seemed almost mechanical.

Sam stayed with her while Michael put through the call. He was scared to say anything to her for fear it would set her off, but he hated the blank way she was looking at him. As if she had already given up.

"Come on, Ma," he said when Michael signaled to him from the front door. He pulled her up to her feet and led her in to the telephone. She took the receiver and put it to her ear without saying anything. Sam heard the priest talking in a low, urgent voice. He and Michael went quietly upstairs.

They found two bottles, one in her suitcase under the bed and one in the top of the closet.

"I hope that's all there is," Michael said as they stood over the sink pouring the liquor out.

"Maybe one day she'll be able to pour it out herself," Sam said. "Or better yet, she won't bring it at all."

"It seems to me we were doing the same thing a year ago," Michael said. "We haven't gotten very far."

"Yes, we have," Sam said slowly. "She didn't take the

drink. She waited until we got home. That's a long way for her to come." He was silent for a minute. "She's very brave," he said softly.

The three of them walked around the lake that evening after they had convinced Ma to eat some dinner. They didn't say much to each other but they all knew some door between them had finally been opened.

"Did you get the new canvas?" Ma asked quietly before they went up to bed.

Sam showed her the roll standing in the corner of the kitchen.

"I want to start a new picture tomorrow," she said as she climbed the stairs. "I've already decided it will be a sunset." She turned and smiled at them. "My first sunset since the Point."